AF555605

Emotional Intelligence

Includes 2 Manuscripts

Emotional Intelligence+ Emotional Intelligence at work

By Lawrence Franz

within this book has been derived from various sources. Please consult a licensed professional before attempting any techniques outlined in this book.

By reading this document, the reader agrees that under no circumstances is the author responsible for any losses, direct or indirect, that are incurred as a result of the use of information contained within this document, including, but not limited to, errors, omissions, or inaccuracies.

Table of Contents

Book 1

Emotional Intelligence

A Guide to Improving Emotion Control and Understanding Relationships

By Lawrence Franz

Introduction

What factors determine the success of an individual in their general life? Could it be powerful cognitive functions? Having a high IQ? There is no concrete answer for this question until you read through this book. In the early days, it was presumed that any individual who exhibited high levels of intelligence would automatically translate to a higher probability being successful. Parents, educators, and peers sang the same tune of high intelligence translating into greater success. We wish it was actually that simple!

If you have the desire of attaining success while living on this earth, you were required to study hard, score good grades, make it to the university, study harder, and graduate with an excellent degree/honors. This path was believed to be the guaranteed shot to a great job and an abundantly successful life.

You spent years believing this notion, and although it's not completely incorrect, it's not the full picture either. Success is the result of a combination of various factors, and the most fundamental of them is your ability to handle your own and other people's emotions.

Emotional intelligence, or emotional quotient, (both represent the same idea), is a type of intelligence that refers to an individual's ability to recognize and manage or control their own and other people's emotions. It is a simple and straightforward concept that comprises two main components:

Identifying or recognizing emotions, intentions, desires, and goals in yourself and other people.

Managing these emotions and actions to accomplish the most positive outcome for everyone involved.

Research on emotional intelligence has been ongoing since the mid-20th century within the psycho-scientific community. However, it wasn't until 1995, when Daniel Goleman published his book by the same name, that emotional intelligence rolled into the mainstream consciousness and became a groundbreaking concept. Back then, intelligence quotient (IQ) was seen as the only factor that mattered when it came to assessing an individual's capabilities. Once emotional intelligence took over, IQ was perceived as a narrow or limited way of assessing an individual's chances of success. The cutthroat world of career, jobs, and business was starkly different from the cushy confines of a classroom.

If one had to navigate the real world, they'd have to adapt to a different kind of intelligence than the academic one used in classrooms or libraries. A person's knowledge and cognitive abilities alone didn't guarantee success in life. A degree didn't automatically mean a high paying job or a profitable business.

At best, you'll get your foot through the door. However, for someone to succeed, you would need much more than just plain intelligence. It would take social, communication, conversation, and emotional skills to raise the bar. These are life skills that aren't taught in the classroom but are learned by living in a hostel, waiting at bars, joining social clubs, being a part of sports teams, and volunteering.

Make a list of ten successful people you admire the most. They are the people you look up to as they lead successful and balanced lives. Are all these folks top honors graduates from distinguished educational institutions with a high IQ? My money is on "No!"

Again, do not let yourself to misunderstand my goal at this point. I am not undermining the importance of intelligence or asking you to shut that book on mechanical engineering and start reading about human psychology. It is awesome if you possess naturally high cognitive abilities and a high intelligence quotient. All I am saying is, you should ideally have both EQ and IQ complementing each other to increase your chances of success in the real world. If you can increase your emotional quotient to back up an already high intelligence quotient, you can achieve many great things!

The objective of this book is to discuss crucial aspects of emotional intelligence and how to use them in your everyday life to make your dream of being successful a reality. We'll take a look at practical techniques to raise your emotional quotient and eventually boost your chances of success.

Chapter 1: Understanding Emotional Intelligence and Models

What is the essence of emotional intelligence? Having the ability to realize your emotions and those of other people who are around you and managing the emotions to get a wonderful and positive outcome.

Essentially, emotional intelligence (EQ) is the knack of perceiving, managing, and evaluating emotions to create the desired positive outcome. John Mayer and Peter Salavoy were the pioneers of emotional intelligence. The term was made popular by Daniel Goleman in 1995 with his groundbreaking book of the same name, *Emotional Intelligence*. However, emotional intelligence as a term was first used by Michael Beldoch in the mid-20th century.

It gives one the capabilities of controlling their feelings and those of others, differentiating emotions in various situations, and controlling the emotional information to drive your actions and what you think. This is a broader and more general definition of emotional intelligence, although there are differences within the scientific community about what it encompasses. The unanimous view is that it is a skill that involves identifying, understanding, and managing emotions.

Emotional Intelligence Ability Model

The emotional intelligence model was created by Mayer and Salovey, who defined emotional quotient as the ability to correctly recognize, evaluate, and generate emotions to facilitate thought, gain a better understanding of emotions, and manage emotions for enhancing both cognitive and emotional development.

The psychologist duo believed that an individual must be assessed on four distinct interconnected abilities to determine their overall EQ. The four abilities are:

Recognizing emotions

This involves picking up verbal and nonverbal clues for understanding a person's emotions.

Reasoning or using these emotions to facilitate thinking and intellectual activity

For example, leveraging emotions to offer solutions or reviewing situations. This helps us focus our limited attention span on the right things and react as per the situation. This benefits the overall creative process.

Understanding emotions

Human emotions are complex. They hold multiple meanings and guide us in understanding another person's emotional state of mind. Emotions give us a chance to understand other people and the emotions they are experiencing. Emotions are full of nuances and cannot be understood from a direct approach. Every emotion holds its own pattern of thoughts, actions, and intentions.

For instance, when an individual undergoes hurtful moments, you may be in a position to determine the reason for the hurting moments. An individual with this particular ability can immediately understand another person's emotional state and why they are thinking or behaving in a certain manner.

Regulating emotions

It involves the capacity of responding to emotions (both yours and those of other individuals) and handling them appropriately. For example, having the ability to contain the situation when another individual is upset or shows emotions of anger. Controlling our own and other people's emotions is a major component of emotional intelligence.

Salovey-Mayer concluded that an individual may be closed to emotional signals that are too painful or uncomfortable while being open to those that aren't overwhelming. This is calculated through the Mayer-Salovey-Caruso Emotional Intelligence Test (MESCEIT). It is measured by emotion-focused problem-solving.

Mixed Model Emotional Intelligence

This model of emotional intelligence was founded on Daniel Goleman's 25 distinct emotional intelligence traits, which encompasses everything from teamwork, service orientation, and accomplishment motivation to self-awareness.

The name mixed model is appropriate since it merges several traits of emotional intelligence with other personality characteristics that are not connected to intelligence and emotion. Emotional competence is a capability that can be learned and developed to create outstanding results. This emotional intelligence model is based on five primary categories, each one with clear emotional competencies:

- **Self-awareness**

Self-awareness is the ability to identify an emotion as we experience it. We tune in to our inner selves for assessing what exactly we are feeling and how to best regulate it. Self-awareness comprises self-confidence in your capabilities and emotional awareness in realizing what you are feeling and the subsequent emotional effects.

People with high self-awareness possess the following competencies:

> They know the emotions they are experiencing and why they are experiencing these emotions.
>
> They recognize how their emotions impact their performance.

They know their weaknesses and strengths.

Self-aware people are open to constructive criticism or feedback, fresher perspectives, constant learning, and personal development.

They are decisive by nature and can make clear decisions even when they're under stress and faced with uncertainties.

People with high self-awareness are able to establish the connection between people's feelings, thoughts, and actions.

They are able to display a sense of humor and view themselves from a lighter perspective. People who indulge in self-deprecating humor are often confident, self-assured, and emotionally intelligent people.

People with high self-awareness do not feel the need to go with the tide. They are happy to stand alone and voice views that do not match popular views.

- **Self-regulation**

Self-regulation is the ability to manage disturbing emotions and emotional impulses that can hinder interpersonal relationships and performance. We think we don't have great control over our emotions, but negative emotions can be managed through various self-regulating techniques like walking, prayer, running, and meditation. To self-regulate effectively, one needs to have control over their impulsive actions, must demonstrate honesty and integrity, possess creative thinking, must be able to handle change easily, and can take responsibility for their actions.

Here are some competencies that people with high self-regulation possess:

> People with high emotional self-control can manage their impulses and disturbing emotions effectively.
>
> They are able to stay calm, positive, and unaffected even in the most trying circumstances.
>
> People with high self-regulation are able to build trust and credibility through reliability, integrity, and authenticity. They are also able to accept their own mistakes and are brave enough to call out others for their unethical acts.
>
> High self-regulation abilities lead these people to meet commitments, keep promises, and act on their word.
>
> They are also highly effective in handling change and adapting to new scenarios.

Motivation

Motivation is the ability to work toward fulfilling a set of goals. The most important aspect of this category is positive thinking. To become a positive thinker, one must always stay positive and be capable of restructuring negative thoughts. This can be accomplished by optimism, commitment, initiative, and drive for achievement. You are perpetually involved in the pursuit of improving yourself to become a better person.

Empathy

Empathy is the ability to not just discern people's emotions but also to "feel" what they feel. Empathy is about understanding others, being able to anticipate other people's needs, helping others develop their qualities, and building relationships with people who are quite different from you. Empathy is comprised of more than a single ability. However, fundamentally, it is about being able to feel and relate to other people's emotions.

People who have high empathy possess the following abilities:

They are extremely perceptive to verbal and nonverbal emotional clues while listening to people.

They show understanding for another person's point of view even though they may not necessarily agree with it.

They are happy to help solve people's problems and concerns in any manner within their capacity.

People with high social awareness acknowledge other people's accomplishments and reward them for their strengths.

Social skills

Relating to other people is another important attribute of emotional intelligence. Social skills are important in teamwork, collaboration, communication, influence, building relationships, and conflict management.

People with high social skills possess the following competencies:

They are able to deal with conflicts in an assertive and straightforward manner.

They embrace open communication and are ready to accept both compliments and criticism.

People with high social skills can inspire others to pursue a shared goal or vision.

Impact of Emotional Intelligence – Examples

Let us say you've been offered constructive feedback by your manager about areas you can improve upon or areas where you didn't perform to your fullest potential. People with a low emotional quotient may take the criticism personally or come up with a host of excuses and blame games to cover their shortcomings. They may not accept their mistakes or they may find a scapegoat to blame their inefficacy on. They may get angry, irritable, depressed, and demotivated. Acting on emotions is easier. Identifying them and regulating them takes work.

Conversely, an individual with greater emotional intelligence will accept the fact that no one is perfect. Rather than taking the feedback personally, they'll introspect about what their manager said and work on areas of improvement to become more efficient. They will stop making similar mistakes. People with a high emotional quotient will actively seek feedback from others rather than focus on proving themselves right. They are less likely to argue and blame others for their shortcomings.

Emotionally intelligent people are open to suggestions and constructive feedback, which eventually helps them accomplish their objectives. For these folks, being right is being more efficient. They value feedback and actively work on it. This is just one of the ways high emotional intelligence can positively affect your productivity and success in the workplace.

Let us now take another example in a personal scenario.

You are involved in a heated discussion about political ideologies with your best friend. While your friend is fervently putting forth their views about their ideology, you firmly stick to your opinion. When they speak, they appear angry. An emotionally intelligent person can quickly gauge this emotion and understand the impact of the topic on their friend. You realize that you could end up hurting or upsetting them if the topic continues for a while.

A person with high emotional intelligence gets a grip on the circumstances easily and gently acknowledges the other person's view even if they don't necessarily subscribe to those ideas. They may not agree with their friend, but they are accepting their right to disagree. Since this person is more thoughtful, empathetic, and sensitive to other people's needs, they can successfully stop a discussion from blowing into a full-fledged fight. Thus, things finish on a constructive and positive note.

Now, consider the same scenario with a person who isn't emotionally intelligent or empathetic toward other people's feelings. This kind of person is adamantly focused on their views. They refuse to understand where the other person is coming from. Thus, the discussion snowballs into a heated argument. They fan the flame of the difference even more. The results are anger, hurt, and negativity. The fight ends badly and affects their interpersonal relationship.

We can all identify that one emotionally intelligent person within our family, friends, or social circle. They always pick the most appropriate thing to say in any situation. They can pacify people, thwart potentially uncomfortable situations, nip arguments in the bud, and arrive at a solution where everyone is pleased. Irrespective of how tricky a scenario is, they manage to find their way through it by using emotional information about their own and other people's feelings.

They excel in handling challenging situations that involve differences between people and know how to assert themselves without offending anyone. These are the empathetic, considerate, and caring folks who also know how to assert themselves. It's no wonder that most companies today demand people with high emotional intelligence for filling leadership positions.

While people with a high intelligence quotient may have the answer or solution to your problems, emotionally intelligent people can make you feel more hopeful about the situation.

Chapter 2: Learn the Difference between Intelligence Quotient and Emotional Quotient

A good intelligence quotient or IQ is helpful for life. Knowing and understanding how to make logical and rational decisions is advantageous to everyone. At the same time, that IQ can only take people so far.

For instance, Jeffrey, a business executive, has a very high IQ. He has thought of many useful ideas for his business, and yet he is unable to get his business to expand or grow. He is having a hard time maintaining his payroll because people are constantly leaving the business.

Why is Jeffrey unable to get his business to grow? He is struggling with his EQ. He is not fully appreciative of his employees. Perhaps he does not understand that they need some balance between their work and their personal lives. This includes issues where workers are not satisfied with their jobs or are feeling too tired or uncomfortable with their work. But Jeffrey does not have the empathy to understand this.

As a result, it becomes hard for even his smartest ideas to thrive and grow. If he had a better EQ, he would make more plans based on what other people need. By adapting his ideas and values around what others want, it would become easier for his business to grow and thrive.

It is through one's EQ that it becomes easier to evolve and change.

What Makes It Different from Personality?

What makes EQ different from a person's standard personality? EQ focuses more on feelings while the personality is all about a person's style.

There are three things that make up every person:

1. The intelligence quotient
2. The emotional intelligence
3. General personality

Personality is hard-wired into one's brain. It is how a person would interact with others and behave in some fashion. Someone's personality can never change

EQ is different as a person can develop it over time. When a person is trained well, it becomes easier for that person to be active and positive. Many points about improving one's EQ will be covered throughout this guide to provide simple ideas for what they can do to get their lives to move forward.

A person's IQ is likely to stay the same throughout one's life. A person has a certain ability to learn things at a specific rate. It might be easier for a person to learn emotions and how to manage them if that person's IQ is not low.

EQ might be related to IQ when all is considered. When a person's EQ is high, it becomes easier for someone to want to learn. That person will use one's IQ to one's advantage. The emotions become balanced so that people fully understand what they can do to grow their lives. As a result, a person will use one's intelligence at a slightly better rate.

The emotional intelligence that a person holds is important for all people who want to accomplish the most in their workplaces.

Chapter 3: The Golden Benefits of Emotional Intelligence

Emotional intelligence is more than just something related to knowing what people feel. It is to understand and recognize what can be done to help others or to at least get along with them.

It is through a person's EQ that someone can get the most out of life. When the level of emotional intelligence of a person is high, their probability of success and enjoying improved work performances is high. There are several positives of one's EQ that must be explored. These points are vital for the workplace in particular as they relate to what people can do to move forward and thrive in their jobs.

Get Along with People

A workplace is often a challenging place. Each person brings their personalities, their biases, and their different levels of intelligence and experience to the work environment. They have to work in harmony and this is not always easy. There is also the added pressure of competition involved. Personal relationships outside of the workplace can also be difficult at times. People often struggle with maintaining friendships. Finding a long-lasting romantic relationship can be challenging to some people.

Those with a high EQ are better equipped to get along with others. A high EQ individual is able to understand the ups and downs that face relationships. They are able come up with smart and clear strategies that will see such conflicts avoided and solving any disagreements amicably.

Become More Productive

With high emotional intelligence, the productivity of such individuals is seen to be of high standards. Those people understand what they want out of their lives and aren't afraid of putting in the effort.

On the other hand, people with a low emotionally intelligent or not at all are unable to take control of their thoughts making them to be less productive. A person might become overly worried when a new task is introduced and it is different from what one might be used to. A person with a low EQ might be afraid of what will happen if a project does not go right. All that worry and fear will cause a person to not do well with a task, thus falling into the trap of not knowing what to do to fix a problem or make things work right.

Stay Accountable

People often shift their responsibilities and try to keep things from being too complicated. They don't want to do things because they resist doing it, or maybe they are not aware of what to do to fix the problems that happen. Others might not be aware of the circumstances surrounding what they are doing.

Accountability is a necessity for people in any workplace. A person who is accountable for one's actions and work is not afraid to accept responsibility for their actions. Maturity of an individual is shown through accountability. It is the measure that provides them with insight of understanding the functions and duties they have to undertake on a daily basis. This includes not only what is done correctly but also any errors that might occur. A person with a strong EQ will be more likely to stay accountable.

Accountability provides a person with the ability to take control of a situation. That person will understand that they are doing something valuable or necessary. By working with the right plans, it becomes easy for a person to stay accountable and confident with what one is going to do with life.

Easier to Manage Risks

There are risks to everything in life. A person might get into a car and drive to the grocery store, but that someone is getting into the risk that the car will malfunction or someone might cause an accident on the road. Meanwhile, a person who plays gridiron football might enjoy playing it, but that individual has the risk of suffering a substantial injury like a concussion.

There are risks involved in every aspect of every workplace. One of the greatest reasons why errors are often made in the workplace is because workers are not fully aware of the risks and what they can do to lessen them. This can cause people to panic when something happens that they did not anticipate. They might not have the emotional fortitude to handle some of the events that occur. Those who can handle and figure out their emotions will have an easier time moving forward and keeping everything under control.

A person's emotional intelligence can be utilized to figure out what one's abilities are and how well certain tasks may be completed. Knowing what can be done to fix issues and having a plan for emergencies is essential.

Avoid Questions

When a person has a low emotional intelligence, they are not certain about the decisions they make. They lack self-confidence. One of the most common questions that a person might ask is what they were thinking about in the past? For instance, a man who made a difficult move in the past might ask himself, "What was I thinking? I can't believe I did something that way. Why did I do that?" That man would have failed to use his emotional intelligence. People make rash decisions when they are not thinking about the results or consequences. They might think about the results that they want to attain, but they never think about why they want it or what they can do to maintain those results.

Emotional intelligence is needed to help people to have faith in what they are deciding to do. People need emotional intelligence to stay comfortable and focused on whatever it is they want to work on. More importantly, there will be less confusion when a person's EQ is strong. That person will not question their own decisions. People with a high EQ will not likely ask questions of other people in the workplace or in other situations. A person who asks lots of questions is revealing their low self-esteem and low self-confidence.

A Matter of Trust

People are loyal to people who they trust. One person might seem to be more intelligent than another, but what if that smarter person is difficult for people to trust? That intelligent person might be seen as stubborn or difficult to work with. An intelligent person might not have the emotional intelligence needed to deal with people. When EQ is missing, that person is not capable of understanding or having empathy toward others. But when a person has a high emotional intelligence, that person becomes easier to trust. This leads to added success and control over any situation.

It is through trust that people can stay positive around others. When people trust each other, they are willing to support one another through anything that might come about in the workplace. Trust focuses on people showing that they recognize each other's emotions and are willing to support each other. People who trust one another are likely to get along and feel better in each other's company.

Without trust, it becomes hard for a business to grow and thrive. More importantly, a personal or romantic relationship will not get off the ground if the people involved do not trust each other.

Managing Customers

An interesting part of working with EQ is that it concentrates on how well people are able to interact with each other in a workplace. This includes working with customers in a smart manner.

It is easier for businesses to grow when its employees have EQ. An employee needs a high EQ to have a sense of empathy with customers. When a person understands the emotions of others it becomes easier for that someone to market a product. Having an understanding of emotions is vital for success. This is especially true of the workplace when customers are involved. Every customer should be treated with respect and care to ensure there are no problems that can't be dealt with.

Let's say that Cherry is working to sell a car. She might notice that a customer is nervous about the process of buying a car. She can empathize with the customer and talk with that person about the process. Cherry might explain what makes a car an attractive investment. She may also identify questions that people have and provide smart answers to those issues. By using her EQ, Cherry is getting in touch with the customer and is showing that she cares about that customer's needs. This will make it easier for her to sell the car to that customer.

It is through the EQs of its employees that relationships with customers can be built. When the employees are capable of working with customers well, it becomes easier for people to feel comfortable with each other while doing business.

Chapter 4: Simple Art of Boosting Your Emotional Self-Awareness

It is of great essence to build your self-awareness as way of achieving high emotional intelligence. This is a wonderful way of giving yourself the full comprehension of your emotions and feelings. You can regulate your emotions for an optimally positive outcome only if you are able to identify these emotions. Labeling emotions and determining your actions based on these emotions is critical to the process of developing emotional intelligence. When you are more aware of your feelings and emotions, recognizing other people's emotions becomes simpler.

Here are solid, proven tips for boosting self-awareness to get you started on the path of emotional intelligence:

Label Your Emotions

Label and categorize your emotions. I know this makes your feelings sound like they belong to a library. However, labeling, or giving names to your emotions, makes it easier to identify and act upon them. When you feel an emotion surging through you, attempt to identify it quickly. Is it fear, insecurity, jealousy, anger, elation, depression, surprise, or a combination of these emotions?

Identify the triggers that cause these emotions. For instance, a specific person may evoke jealousy in you because you feel they are more successful than you.

Why do you experience certain emotions? What are the triggers that anger or hurt you? What makes you happy and sad? What is the source of positive and destructive emotions in you? Labeling your feelings and recognizing the stimuli for various emotions will increase your emotional self-awareness.

Grab a pen and paper to list your emotions when you experience a compelling feeling. Mention the precise emotion or feeling that you are experiencing. Accompany this emotional label with the trigger that caused it. What is it that made you feel the way you do? When you recognize an emotion, it is easier to manage it.

For instance, let us assume you feel a deep sense of loathing for a person without any specific reason. You dislike them and can't stand them, but funnily, can't tell why you dislike them. Upon closer examination of your feelings, you realize you dislike them because you are envious of them. You may believe they are always having a wonderful life, while things never go your way. By nailing this emotion as jealousy, you can regulate your potentially negative emotions.

Once you recognize the emotion as irrational jealousy, you will view it in a more logical and understanding manner. You'll begin to think along the lines that it isn't really someone's fault that they lead an amazing life. In fact, they should be applauded for working hard toward their goals. You'll realize that no one has a perfect life. Everyone goes through shares of trials and tribulation to attain success, which isn't necessarily visible to the outside world. Sometimes, it is only how we perceive things and not the reality. Thus, once you are more mindful of your emotions, you can work with them more positively.

Be an Expert on Yourself

What is the one thing you should do to bring about changes in your thoughts, actions, and behavior? The answer is: awareness about these thoughts and subsequent actions! To make changes, you ought to know what you have to improve upon.

Knowing yourself inside out is the key to being more emotionally aware and savvy. Did you know athletes are trained to identify and overcome feelings before an important upcoming game? If you are able to identify and take full control of the emotions that you experience, your productivity won't be affected.

Go back and think about all the recent instances where you let emotions get the better of you and affect your productivity. Haven't you let trivial matters impact your performance?

By being aware of your strengths and weaknesses, it is easier to confidently accomplish your objectives. There is a lesser scope for frustration, low productivity, and disappointment. Self-confidence increases your assertiveness while you express your thoughts and opinions, which is important for developing social skills.

Once you gain greater awareness, you will rarely be ruled by emotions. You have a clear edge if you are able to regulate your emotions. An emotionally aware person stops being a victim of their emotions and uses these emotions in a positive way to reach a desired outcome.

Spend Time Recognizing Areas of Development to Strengthen Them

- List all your strengths and weaknesses.
- Take a formal, psychological personality assessment test that helps you discover your own skills, abilities, limitations, and values.
- Obtain objective feedback from people you trust.

One way that works wonders for increasing your self-awareness is journaling. Write in a flowing stream of consciousness about the thoughts you are feeling and experiencing as they are occurring. What are the emotions you are experiencing? How do you react to the feelings physiologically? Are you experiencing a faster heartbeat, sweaty palms, increased pulse, and so on?

Emotions aren't always straightforward. In fact, they are complex and multilayered. For example, you may have a heated argument with your partner and feel angry, hurt, upset, and vengeful all at the same time. Write emotions exactly as you are experiencing them, even if two emotions appear to contradict each other. For instance, if you've got a scholarship to study overseas, you may be elated at the opportunity. However, the thought of leaving behind your partner may cause a twinge of sadness, too. You are acknowledging and validating your emotions by writing them.

Make a list of every role you play in your daily life such as being a parent, sibling, volunteer, worker, and more. What are the emotions linked with each role? For example, you may enjoy your role as a parent, but you can also be an unhappy employee. Examine every role and the emotions attached to it carefully.

Naming emotions linked to every relationship will help you manage emotions within that relationship more efficiently. It will keep you in greater control of your emotional reaction where the specific role is concerned.

Do a Frequent Check-In

Do a frequent check-in with your emotions much like how you have a waiter checking in with you frequently to know if you need anything. You do a mental check-in of your emotions periodically to understand how you are feeling at different times during the day. It is a sort of, "Hello, mind, how are you feeling? What can be done to make you feel better?"

Examine where the specific feelings come from. Are you feeling low and deflated because your boss said something to you in the morning? Are you feeling angry and hurt because you fought with your partner? Are you experiencing certain physiological symptoms as a result of these emotions or feelings? Are these emotions impacting your body language, posture, gestures, and expressions? Are these emotions evident or visible to others? Are you more transparent when it comes to expressing your emotions? Are your decisions primarily determined by emotions?

If you want to be a more emotionally balanced person, reconnect with your primary emotions, recognize them, accept the emotions, and use them for making better decisions.

Use Third Person

Research in the field of labeling our emotions has indicated that when we distance ourselves from our emotions, or view them more objectively, we gain higher self-awareness. Next time you feel the urge to say, "I am disappointed," try to say, "Andrew is disappointed."

If that seems too preposterous, try saying, "I am presently experiencing sadness," or, "One of my feelings at the moment is sadness."

These are techniques through which you are distancing yourself from overpowering emotions to stay naturally composed. You are basically treating your emotions as just another piece of information rather than being overwhelmed by them.

Each time you find yourself experiencing an urge to react to a situation, take a moment to name it. Then use it in the third person to distance yourself from intense emotions.

Emotions Don't Always Need to be Fixed

You don't always have to identify emotions with the intention of fixing them. Self-awareness is not about fixing emotions. It is about recognizing these emotions and letting them pass rather than allowing them to get the better of you. Society has conditioned us to think that certain emotions are bad. We mistakenly believe that experiencing these emotions makes us a bad person.

Far from it, emotions aren't good or bad. They are just that, emotions. There's no need to push away the seemingly bad emotions. Acknowledge that you are experiencing an emotion by saying something like, "I am experiencing jealousy." Practice deep breathing for a while until the emotion passes. Rather than pushing the emotion away and, in the process, increasing its intensity to come back even stronger, gently acknowledge it and let it be until it passes.

It takes around six seconds for the body to absorb chemicals that can alter your emotions. Give your body that much time.

We often share a hostile relationship with our emotions. They are believed to be something that is negative and should be fought or suppressed. However, emotions are information that helps us function in our daily lives. Overcome the mindset that emotions are good or bad, and instead focus on using them to empower you. Rather than letting emotions take control of you, use emotional information to work with them.

Emotions are neural hormones that are released as a direct response to our perceptions regarding the world. They direct us toward a specific action. All emotions have a distinct message and objective, which means there's no such thing as a good or bad emotion.

For example, fear helps us focus on an impending danger and take the necessary action to defend ourselves. Similarly, sadness makes us experience a sense of loss and facilitates a better understanding of what we truly care about.

If you move away from your best friend and become sad, this means you truly care about them so much that you experienced sadness. This is valuable information. Hence, sadness is not a bad emotion. It can determine the things or people that mean a lot to you.

If you use emotions as information for recognizing feelings, they can be channeled positively. The number one rule for developing higher emotional intelligence is to stop judging and curbing your emotions.

Train Yourself to Identify Emotions Based on Physiological Reactions

Our emotions often have physical manifestations. For example, you may feel anxious before a job interview or an important presentation. You experience the sensation of having "butterflies in your stomach" before addressing an audience on the stage.

Don't you find your heart pounding with excitement when you are about to go on a date with someone you've fancied for long? Nervousness leaves us with sweaty palms and stiff muscles.

While these are only some of the physiological reactions we experience with our emotions, research has proven that a variety of emotions are strongly associated with stimulating certain parts of the body.

Regular patterns of physical sensations are linked with each of the six fundamental emotions, including fear, happiness, anger, sadness, disgust, and surprise. Human emotions discreetly overlap physiological sensations. For example, lower limb sensations are associated with sadness. Similarly, increased upper limb sensations are connected with anger. A strong feeling of disgust generates sensations within the throat and digestive system. Fear and surprise generate sensations in the chest.

Identify Recurring Patterns

This can be one of the most effective parts of knowing yourself. Neuroscience will help you understand the process more effectively. Our brains have an inherent tendency to follow established neural paths rather than creating new ones. This doesn't necessarily mean that the established patterns are serving us positively or that they can't be altered.

For instance, when a person becomes angry, they may bottle up their emotion rather than express it. This has become an emotional pattern with the person and is deeply embedded in the mind. However, awareness of this pattern can help the person chart another course of action, where the person practices responding instead of simply reacting to the emotion. However, the first step to charting a new pattern is identifying a pattern.

Recognize the build-up of emotions before something suddenly triggers you. These triggers have a predictable pattern. If you are already frustrated, you are more likely to see a situation in a more negative light. Similarly, if you are overcome by fear, you are more likely to interpret a stimulus as a threat. Come up with a pattern that is predictable and be in the know of such biases and their effects towards your emotions. The more efficient you become in recognizing your biases, the lower your chances of misinterpreting a stimulus.

Work with What You Know about Emotions

Emotions are important pieces of data that help you gauge things from a clearer and objective perspective. Don't suppress, ignore, fight, or feel overwhelmed by your emotions. Instead, you should build a valuable library of experiences with them. The purpose of emotional awareness is to concentrate our attention on these emotions and use them positively to create the desired outcome.

Treat your emotions as data that relies on your view of the world, or as a guide on how to act. When you open yourself to this data, you enjoy access to a huge resource of emotions that can be utilized to drive your actions in the right direction. With a defined emotional route, you will find it easy to know where you have to move and reach as intended. Therefore, you should acknowledge and recognize your emotions as data, and work with them instead of trying to beat them.

Begin by carefully noticing how you feel at the moment. Observe emotions without judging them or attempting to fix them. Learn to simply notice your emotions.

Be open to Feedback and Constructive Criticism

If you wish to build a great awareness channel of your emotions, then you need to welcome any feedback and criticism emanating from other individuals. For instance, a friend may tell you that each time they talk about their accomplishments they sense your pangs of envy or dislike toward them. This may help you tune into your emotions and emotional triggers more effectively.

Emotionally intelligent folks are open to receiving feedback, and they always consider the other person's point of view. You may not necessarily agree with them, but listening to other people's criticism and feedback helps you work on your blind spots. This can help you recognize your thoughts, triggers, and behavioral patterns.

I know a person who, in a bid to increase his self awareness and emotional quotient, actively goes around asking people for feedback about his words, feelings (as they understand it), and actions. It acts as an emotion meter, which helps him gain greater awareness of his emotions and regulate them more efficiently.

Chapter 5: Calmly Manage Your Stress

Stress decreases your ability to control your emotions. When you're stressed, you're more likely to feel anxious and depressed. You'll have mood swings.

Stress keeps you from tuning in to your negative emotions and from practicing any of the things we have discussed in this book.

When you are stressed and not in a position to manage it, it becomes hard to recognize the emotions at work; neither will you be able to think about them before acting on them. More so, you would acutely avoid your negative emotions. This prevents you from experiencing them and becoming conversant with them. Therefore, it is important that you carve out a method to manage stressful situations. The most important thing when you are stressed is to remember to be calm and to detach as much as possible, usually progressively, from the source of the stress. Sometimes, this could even be people.

Practice Mindfulness

Mindfulness is a very important tool for enhancing emotional intelligence. It is the ability to be emotionally present in the moment without judgment. To practice mindfulness, you must focus your attention on the emotions you are feeling and the signals they are sending into your environment including how they affect any interactions you might be having.

You must also not judge your emotions. Allow them to manifest. That is like saying "feel them." This is so that you can recognize them. Do not suppress them. Take notice of the emotional buildup of the person you are interacting with too before deciding whether or not to act on your own emotions.

Chapter 6: Solid Steps to Improve Interpersonal Connection

We've established in earlier chapters how emotional intelligence is the master key to effective leadership and social skills. By tuning into other people's emotions or by empathizing with how they feel, there is a higher chance that you will respond appropriately to create the desired positive result. Thus, our ability to connect with our own and other people's emotions can be a powerful tool in social and leadership situations.

Understanding other people, helping overcome stress situations, motivating your team, negotiating business deals, and building a close-knit social circle becomes easier when you can use the emotional information you have about them as leverage. It increases situational awareness and our ability to read people, thus helping us make the most positive decision.

Here are some verbal and nonverbal factors impacting social-emotional quotient, or our ability to read and deal with people:

Body Language

Research reveals that body language accounts for 50 percent of our communication. You'd wonder why there were words in the first place if body language accounts for half the communication process. Tuning in to a person's body language will help you pick up important signals related to their emotional state and subconscious thoughts or feelings.

Here's a quick cue sheet to reading people's feelings through their body language:

- Crossed arms and legs are signals of people creating a subconscious barrier. They are emotionally closed, suspicious, or do not subscribe to your ideas. They aren't open to listening to your views or are disinterested in the topic of conversation. You may have to emotionally open the person up a bit by changing the topic and then get back to the original topic. The physical act of uncrossing their arms and legs will make them more subconsciously receptive to your ideas.

- How can you tell a genuine smile from a fake one? Simple, it's all in the eyes. Observe that there's crinkled skin near the person's eyes forming crow's feet. People often present a happy expression to hide their true feelings. However, if their smile doesn't cause the skin around their eyes and mouth to crinkle, they are most likely not as happy as they are pretending to be. Artificial smiles create wrinkles only around the mouth, while genuine smiles create wrinkles around the sides of the eyes.

- When people constantly take their gaze away from you while speaking, they are most likely not being very honest or trying to hide something. Similarly, if a person speaks to you without taking their gaze away from you for long, they may be trying to threaten or intimidate you with their gaze. It is alright to look away periodically. However, shifting gaze constantly is a red flag.

- When you are addressing a group of people, closely observe the ones who are nodding excessively or in a more exaggerated manner. These are the people who are most concerned about your approval. They are anxious about making a positive impression and want to be in your "good books."

- People who are nervous or anxious tend to fidget with their hands or objects. Other signs of nervousness also include excessive blinking, tapping feet, and constantly running one's hand over the face.

- When an entire group walks into the room, how do you analyze who the leader or decision maker is? Quickly observe everyone's posture. The leader will most likely walk with a straight posture, with shoulders pulled out. Subconsciously, they are trying to occupy maximum space to convey authority over their team. Standing straight and pulling back shoulders increases a person's physical frame. It makes them come across as much bigger than they actually are. This is why people in power love to keep this posture to show their influence over a group or place.

- Expressions are the windows into a person's emotional state. When a person is amazed or surprised, their eyebrows are raised, and the upper eyelids widen. Similarly, the mouth gapes open. Expressions can often overlap, so watch for microexpressions that can reveal precise emotions.

- For instance, raised eyebrows can also reveal fear. Look for other micro expression clues to determine the exact emotion. If a person is experiencing fear, the eyebrows will be raised and pulled together with tensed lower eyelids, while the two corners of their lips will appear stretched. Similarly, a person's surprise is expressed by eyebrows pulled up and a lowered jaw. Learn to read the entire face, especially microexpressions, if you want to learn more about how a person is feeling.

- Since microexpressions occur in fractions of seconds, they are virtually impossible to fake. For instance, notice how when people are being deceptive, their mouths will slightly angle differently. Similarly, their eye movements become more rapid, the nostrils flare a little bit, and they purse their lips together (a subconscious gesture signaling their lips are sealed, or they won't reveal the truth). Since these split expressions are driven by the subconscious, this makes them involuntary, and it is almost impossible to manipulate them.

- Enlarged pupils reveal intense emotions such as excitement, elation, delight, surprise, and interest. When a person is attracted to you or truly delighted to see you, their pupils will involuntarily enlarge.

- The direction of a person's feet can also determine what's going on in their mind. Since feet aren't the first thing on anyone's mind, it's harder to manipulate body language related to legs and feet. If a person's feet are pointing away from you, they are subconsciously signaling their need to escape. However, if their feet are pointed toward you, they are interested or in agreement with what you are saying.

- Typical signs of frustration and stress are clenched jaws, wrinkled eyebrows, and tensed neck. The person's words notwithstanding, if you observe any of these signs, he or she may be undergoing a stressful situation that they are trying to conceal. The trick for reading people's emotions accurately is to keep an eye out for a clear mismatch between verbal and nonverbal clues.

- Observe a person's walk to tune in to their feelings. People with a heavier gait along with low gravity while moving their legs are most likely hurt, stressed, frustrated, or depressed. People who walk with a slower and more relaxed pace are reflecting upon something. Notice how confident, happy, and goal-oriented people walk swiftly in one direction.

- Observing a person's eye movements is a near accurate way of gauging how they are feeling since our eye movements are connected to precise brain functions. Our eye movements have an established pattern depending on the brain function or type of information we are trying to access. For instance, if an individual is caught in an internal conflict or dilemma (to either speak the truth or lie), there is a likelihood that they will tend to look towards their left collarbone. Darting sideways from one side to another can be a red flag that indicates deception.

- Proxemics is a subtopic within body language that talks about how people reveal their feelings and emotions through the physical distance they maintain with other people during the process of face-to-face interaction or communication. It is a very useful nonverbal signal for understanding a person's thought process or state of mind.

Psychologists and body language experts believe that the amount of physical distance we maintain while interacting with a person helps establish the dynamics of our relationship with them or reveals our emotions about them.

A person who isn't standing very close to you may not be emotionally open or receptive to you. They may have a tendency to closely guard their emotions or give only a little of themselves to the interaction. Such people may be more emotionally guarded and closed. You may need to make extra effort to get them to drop their guard and feel less intimidated. It may be a defense mechanism against being emotionally hurt or vulnerable.

On the other hand, if a person is leaning in your direction, they may subconsciously convey being emotionally open, or they trust you with their feelings. They may also be more interested in what you are speaking about.

Tone

The tone, volume, pitch, and emphasis of a person's voice can help you decode the hints that can help you tell what they are feeling. For example, if you notice plenty of inconsistencies in the tone of their voice as they speak, they are probably very angry, hurt, excited, or nervous. Ever notice how your voice shakes when you speak in a rage or are nervous about something? It can also be a sign the person is lying.

Similarly, if a person is speaking louder or softer than their regular volume, something may be amiss. Again, a person's tone is a dead giveaway. Sometimes people say something that sounds like a compliment. However, upon examining their tone closely, you realize the sarcasm and the condescension with which it was uttered.

The tone in which an individual ends their sentence says a lot about what they are trying to convey even with similar verbal clues. For example, if a person completes their sentence on a raised note, they are doubtful of something or are asking a question. Similarly, if they finish the sentence with a flat tone, they are pronouncing a statement or judgment. Watch out for how people end their sentences to get a clue about their inner feelings.

Again, the words people emphasize can help you uncover their true feelings. For instance, if an individual gets to say, "Have you borrowed the blazer?" while emphasizing "borrowed," it indicates their doubt over whether you have borrowed, stolen, or done something else to the blazer. However, if the emphasis is on "you," they aren't sure if it is you or someone else who has borrowed the blazer.

I also like to look at pauses between phrases to know about the person's attitude, emotions, and intentions. For example, if a person pauses after saying something, it could be because what they just said is extremely important to them, or they truly believe in it. Sometimes, a person pauses to seek validation or feedback from others. The speaker wants to gauge your reaction to what they said since it is important for them.

When people are in a more emotionally unstable or negative frame of mind (angry, hurt, or upset), their voice tends to be higher pitched or squeaky. They are most likely losing a grip on their emotions or aren't able to regulate their emotions effectively. Notice how, when people are very angry, their voice becomes more screechy and squeaky, as if they are about to cry.

The Speed of a Speech

A person's emotions clearly impact the speed of their speech. Notice how you start talking much faster than your normal rate of speech, or words per minute, when you are angry or upset. A rapid speech can convey lack of organization, uncertainty, or lack of clarity. The person is not very comfortable with speaking and is just trying to finish throwing their words. Again, a slower than usual pace translates into low self-confidence, inability to express emotions, inability to come to terms with one's emotions, lack of emotional reassurance, and other similar feelings.

Verbal Clues

A person's choice of words can say a lot about what they are thinking and feeling. Words are symbolic of our thoughts and feelings which, when combined with nonverbal clues, give us a comprehensive understanding of their emotional state.

The brain we have as humans is a miracle that one cannot unravel. When we think, or process rational and logical thoughts, we tend to use nouns and verbs. Conversely, when we attempt to express our thoughts or feelings in a verbal or written format, there is a tendency to use more adverbs and adjectives.

Any basic sentence features a subject and a verb. For example, "I walked." When a person adds more words to it, they can indicate their feelings or personality. For example, "I walked fast," can indicate a sense of urgency, fear, or insecurity. There are clear reasons why people use specific words over others.

Similarly, there is a hidden meaning behind what people say. Through their choice of words, people reveal emotions left unsaid.

Let's say you booked a table to take your family out for dinner at one of the fanciest, fine dining restaurants that recently opened in your neighborhood. The server greets you courteously and directs you to your table. What follows is an amazing dining experience.

The waiter introduces each of the seven courses in an informative yet engaging style, while you dine and enjoy wine in an upscale ambiance. After you enjoy a hearty meal and call for the tab, the waiter inquires if you enjoyed the food. You reply with, "The entrées were good."

The waiter doesn't look very delighted, even if what you said is a compliment in your opinion. Those four words you uttered reveal your real opinion about the food. It implies that other than the entrées, everything else was pretty average or the only thing that stood out during the entire meal were the entrées.

Did you actually say everything else other than the entrées was average? No. Then why did the waiter look crestfallen at your statement? It true that many individuals pass a lot of information through what they said and unsaid things. Gather the hidden meaning or subtext behind what people say to tune in to their inner feelings. Notice how sometimes people will say, "You look very lovely today." It can either mean you look plain every day (which is a more passive-aggressive kind of statement), or you are looking exceptionally good today compared to other days.

Another powerful clue about what people are thinking or feeling is noticing how they talk about other people. A number of researchers discovered that merely asking participants to rate positive and negative traits of three other people revealed a lot about the participants' social competence, general well-being, other people's perception of them, and their mental health.

It was observed that an individual's inclination to view other people in a positive manner was a strong indication of their own positive emotions. There is a strong link between seeing others in a more positive light and being emotionally stable, happy, productive, and enthusiastic.

On the other hand, viewing others in a negative light bears a strong correlation with a general sense of dissatisfaction, low self-esteem, anti-social behavior, and narcissism. People who hold plenty of negative emotions tend to perceive other people in a poorer or more negative light. This can also be an indication of emotional issues, mental health conditions, or a personality disorder. Again, emotions aren't good or bad but are reflections of how you are feeling. If a person experiences more negative emotions for others around them, it can be a clue to how they really feel about themselves.

If a person says that they "made up their mind" after plenty of deliberation, the phrase indicates a mindset that is high on logic and rational thinking. The individual may be more contemplative and practical by nature. They may examine all the options available before arriving at a particular decision. These are not your likely contenders for a snap of the moment decisions.

Do you know what metalanguage is? It is the intended words behind the words you speak. You don't say something directly but reveal it through the words you use. For example, notice how when people want to get someone to agree with what they've said, they'll always place yes, done, or okay followed by a question mark at the end. For example, "I can't hand in the project today. I'll submit it tomorrow, okay?" It is like manipulating the other person to agree.

To further increase your social-emotional quotient, pay attention to the sounds people utter, other than coherent words. Moaning, grunting, sighing, and so on, can reveal a lot. Sometimes, these sounds will complement the words the speaker is using to make the message even more persuasive. However, at other times, there may be a mismatch between the person's words and sounds.

For example, someone may say, "I am having a really good day," followed by a sigh, which can indicate they are simply being sarcastic and are in fact having a bad day. You can even understand more about what a person really means when you observe their words and other miscellaneous sounds they make.

Environmental Clues

A person's immediate environment says a lot about their emotional state. For instance, a messy, unclean, or disorganized space can indicate a lack of clarity of emotions or thoughts. Of course, everything has to be analyzed within a context. Someone may have an unkempt house because they are too busy to tidy it up and doesn't have housekeeping help.

All of us have certain spaces around us that are inaccessible that we don't really bother cleaning or organizing (space behind the cupboard or under the bed). These are spaces that we wouldn't normally clean. If such spaces are immaculately clean or organized, it can indicate anxiety or a disorder (obsessive-compulsive disorder).

Well-organized and clean spaces can indicate clarity of emotions or control over one's emotions. The person tends to be more reflective and introverted by nature. Similarly, people who are outwardly focused, or extroverts, tend to be surrounded by chaos.

This isn't pop psychology, but it is based on clear principles of how the environment around us is created through our actions, which themselves are directed by our subconscious thoughts and emotions. For example, using bright, vibrant, and bold prints in your décor or attire can be a sign of confidence, emotional self-assurance, and independence of thought or opinion. Likewise, a home with brighter and more vibrant colors is an indication of being bold, emotionally expressive, and outgoing. These people are not afraid of taking risks and are more than capable of understanding the needs and feelings of other people. More subtle colors imply inward directed emotions, or an introverted personality. These people may not be too receptive to another person's feelings and emotions.

People who hold on to old objects or hoard various objects can be excessively emotional, sensitive, or sentimental. They find it tough to move away from their past emotions or are still ridden by feelings of shame, regret, and guilt related to the past. These are people who latch on to old memories and can't release the emotions that hold them back.

When you use these verbal and nonverbal principles to understand people, your social-emotional quotient invariably increases.

Chapter 7: Emotional Intelligence and Relationships

Our relationships are our support system. A vital road to success is being able to recognize harmful relationships and discarding them accordingly. Also, you must be able to categorize your relationships and know which ones build you up the most.

Do you wish that your relationship was better or closer? If so, you don't need to visit a therapist for couples. Instead, you can improve your relations by applying emotional intelligence to the mix. We've gone over what the term means: using your feelings and moods to effectively live your life and have a positive impact. There are exercises as outlined in this book that will help you manage your emotions and gain the skills needed to help you interact with other people in a better way.

How can EQ Improve your Relationship?

No matter what problem you are facing in your relationship, you can improve it. As we've already mentioned in previous chapters, people with high emotional intelligence enjoy success in more areas than people who don't, and close relationships are no exception to this. Think about it this way: does anyone ever think about leaving their marriage because they have a partner who is too attentive, too understanding, or too encouraging and supportive? Once you apply EQ to the relationship you have with your partner, you can miraculously transform it. But where should you begin?

Building up Awareness in your Relationship

A high awareness of self will let you know what emotional factors you need in order to thrive and be happy. For a relationship to thrive and be happy, however, you and your significant other need to become aware of which emotional factors are needed so you can help each other meet your needs. The reason why people get into relationships in the first place is because these factors were being met when the relationship began.

Necessary Emotional Factors and How to Find Them

But the factors we need to thrive and grow are always changing, meaning that having EQ here refers to staying aware of those factors and whether they are being met on both sides. As soon as partners can sense that their relationship is helping them to grow into a better person, they will want to continue it. Here are the steps to doing this:

- **Make a List of the Emotional Factors you Need**: Here you will write down the top three emotional factors needed for you to feel fulfilled in a relationship. Have your partner do the same.

- **Make a List of the Factors you think They Need:** Now you will write down what you believe are the top three emotional factors needed by your partner in order to feel fulfilled. Have them also make a list for you.

- **Trade Lists:** Now you will trade lists and each read them and have a discussion afterward. This is a good way to generate fresh ideas to meet the required emotional factors for each of you.

Identifying and Managing Emotions in your Relationship

Important results from research on emotions has proven that they play a direct role in how well (or poorly) people perform. Certain feelings like anxiety or anger can nourish or stand in the way of relationships, while feelings such as optimism, enthusiasm, and confidence have a tendency to make them more productive. One emotion that nearly always gets in the way and has long-term negative effects is depression. What this implies is that relationships able to handle anxiety or anger in a positive way and that stay away from depression and nurture optimism, enthusiasm, and confidence will become healthier and more rewarding.

Why You Should Know about Contagious Emotions

Managing feelings in a relationship is difficult. It's the landscape that happens as a result of you and your partner's feelings that involves the contagion of emotions. This refers to the fact that feelings are similar to a virus in how they can spread between people. You can actually catch the anxiety, depression, or anger of your partner, or you can infect your loved one with your own enthusiasm and confidence.

How to Use this Phenomenon to your Advantage

In order to use this phenomenon to benefit your relationship, you have to know how to manage the feelings that are influencing your relations. Here are some skills you can work on for this.

- **Learn how to Relax at Will:** If you can make yourself relax at will, it shows that you know how to regulate your feelings. This will let you become immunized against negative emotions from your partner, letting you keep perspective, which has a tendency to get lost when both partners are in a bad state of mind. Negative feelings like depression or anxiety will heighten your feeling arousal and lead to a rigidity in your mental state, making it harder to act productively and accurately interpret what is happening. This can lead to a loud argument or one of you storming away.

- **The Benefit of Regulating your Emotions:** But when both of you learn how to regulate these feelings, you can stay rational and calm, making accurate assessments of what is happening and freeing yourself from the negative impact of another's feelings. You don't need to shout back when your partner shouts at you or catch their anxiety when they are fretting about bills. You should stay calm in such emotions to foster your relationship to a better zone amid any challenges.

- **Practice Exercises for Relaxation Together:** Every day for the following eight weeks, start practicing exercises for relaxation with your loved one. You will find that this helps both of you manage your feelings instead of letting them drive you apart.

These tips, along with the key points in the last chapter, will help you guide your relationship to a better place. Building awareness in your relationship and working against catching emotions like fear, anxiety, or anger from each other is a great first step to take.

Chapter 8: Creative Summary of Building Self-Confidence

Emotionally intelligent people are self-confident in nature. They have confronted their innermost demons and have emerged victorious. It is essential to be self-confident in order to be emotionally intelligent. In this chapter, we will discuss how we can become more confident of ourselves through four easy methods.

Identify Your Weaknesses

The first step in the journey of becoming self-confident is becoming aware of the self. The foremost task for anyone who wants to become self-confident is to identify their weaknesses. These are areas of your life that make you unsure of yourself. It can be your personality trait or a physical trait. Always remember there is no such weakness that one cannot overcome. All it takes is hard work and dedication. Most people do not correctly identify their weakness and the areas that make them feel insecure of themselves and, as a result, suffer from a demotivated attitude in their lives. Becoming self-confident helps one make better decisions in life and achieve success without any ado. It is essential that you familiarize yourself with your shortcomings. It is no good living in denial or with an escapist attitude. You can run from your demons but cannot break free until you confront them head-on.

Plan Out Your Course of Action

Having once identified your problem areas, chalk out a course of action upon which you will act. Set aside a fixed amount of time from your daily schedule where you will single-mindedly address your concerns. If it is losing weight then you will exercise for that period of time not concerning yourself with other mortal affairs of this life. Unless such dedication is shown, change remains a distant dream for most of us. Do not set very lofty targets for they demotivate you from the very start. Set yourself realistic and manageable targets that you can foresee yourself achieving in a relatively short time span. Most people do not even initiate this change required to gain self-confidence.

Act Upon It

Having once identified your weaknesses, it becomes the time to act upon them. You must not be hesitant of a lifestyle change or a mental makeover because once you decide to overcome your weaknesses, your life will change for certain. Most people remain snugly wrapped up in the cocoon of their comfort zones and don't want to step out and sweat it out. It is essential to remember that you will have to endure much in order to change the way you are. It won't come to you while you are relaxing on your couch. Be it losing fat or gaining muscle, be it succeeding in an examination or in a real-life relationship, unless you work toward it, you will achieve nothing. Hence, do not hesitate to act once having familiarized yourself with your shortcomings.

Reward Yourself

Rewards are an imperative to work harder and with more dedication. Unless you reward yourself along with your journey of transformation, the journey will appear too arduous to complete. Rewards in no way mean stepping out of the line and deviating yourself from your goal but just a little token of pampering. This little reward gives you further motivation and keeps you going. This is to show that you love yourself and appreciate all the efforts that you are making in order to induce a lifestyle change.

Conclusion

There is a wide variety of people in our modern society. Some are high achievers, others are moderate achievers or average people. What is the determining factor making the individuals to be different? What is the factor for fulfillment? More and more people are coming to realize that there is something which differentiates people and that most of it can be developed. More and more people are keying into their emotional intelligence and their positive intelligence to achieve fulfillment. We have highlighted these important concepts in this book and we know that a careful practice of the principles embedded in this book will result in mind-boggling achievement. We hope you experience it in your life.

Emotional intelligence gives you the capacity to tackle a number of challenging circumstances. You will also find that as you meditate on a daily basis, your intuition will truly become honed. There is a very good reason to want to do this as well. Over the course of your life, you have been programmed by everything that happened in your life. If you watch TV, you get programmed into believing that certain products add to your lifestyle. If you watch too much TV of a mindless nature, you tend to become mindless and this exercise once a day will help you to come back into the real world and find the reality of life is actually much simpler than you may imagine.

I wish you well in your journey and would suggest you read the book several times and implement the suggestions made within its pages to improve your levels of emotional intelligence and start to life a life full of joy and fulfilment.

Emotional Intelligence at Work

A Self-Help Guide That Teaches You to Build Your Social Skills and Establish Strong Relationships with Your Peers

By: Lawrence Franz

Table of Contents

Introduction

Thank you for downloading *Emotional Intelligence*. Workplace stress is one of the worst health problems plaguing the modern world, accounting for 12.5 million work days lost in the United States alone as of 2016. Workplace stress also causes many physical and mental health problems. Among these are migraines, heightened blood pressure and heart rate, chronic anxiety, and paranoia, to name a few. Within the following chapters, we will go over some of the more useful methods of handling emotions within the workplace, and day-to-day life as well.

There are many facets of emotional intelligence that are extremely useful in the workplace that are often ignored. All too many people take new jobs, gain bad relationships with their coworkers, do not try to resolve their issues, and flee promptly. This hardly works in the short term and never works in the long term. If tools to handle emotions are never gained, then the same issues are always going to arise despite the workplace or living situation. If you have problems with working, then why not solve the problem at its source—your emotions?

This book will feature advice on a number of topics: improving interpersonal connections at work, controlling emotions, building confidence, finding long-lasting success, social engineering, and leadership. In all of these subjects, the reader should find at least one thing to take away from all this. Emotional intelligence is not something which should be underestimated. It can be one of the most important traits that a person can have or develop throughout life.

There are many great books on the market covering this subject. Thank you again for downloading this one. Enjoy!

Chapter One: Improving Interpersonal Connections at Work

A workplace can often be a demanding, high-stress environment to find oneself in. All this pressure can be amplified even higher when interpersonal connections are either not being made or are in bad conditions in the workplace. This is why it is of the utmost importance to improve the relationships one has with their coworkers and to keep improving on them continually. In this chapter, we will look at some useful tips and techniques for improving relationships with coworkers and working more effectively within group settings.

The first step in improving relationships with coworkers would have to be a check on your own workplace stressors. Before trying to fix what is going on with other workers, it is important to try to fix whatever is going on with you. To manage stress from the outward would be to hit the bullseye on the wrong target. Some of the most common workplace stressors that plague most modern employees are excessive workloads, low salaries, work that is not challenging or engaging, lack of opportunity for enhancement or growth, lack of social support, unclear performance expectations or conflicting demands, and lack of control over job-related decisions. Odds are that, if you are employed, one or more of these stressors apply to you. There is no shame in this, in fact, it is the norm, with around 65% of Americans citing their top source of stress as being work.

This epidemic of workplace stress is especially problematic because of its effects on the health and well-being of workers. Short-term stress is one thing, causing stomach aches, headaches, sleep disturbances, difficulty concentrating, and short temper. It is long-term stress, however, that causes the more dire effects, such as insomnia, anxiety, high blood pressure, and immune system weakening. This is where stress becomes very dangerous and potentially deadly. Most do not deal with their stress until it becomes a problem, but once it does, it may already be too late. This is why it is important to apply skills in coping with workplace stress.

One way of coping with workplace stress is to keep track of your stressors throughout the day. This can be done easily through journaling your inner thoughts throughout the day. Another way is to respond to stress in healthy ways. Rather than coping with unhealthy comfort foods, alcohol, or tobacco, you could try exercising, practicing one of your hobbies, or trying something new whenever you start to feel stressed out. Taking periods of rest is another important one that many neglect to do in these times, but effective working is just not possible without an occasional break. To work constantly is to build up a house on foundations of sand. Meditation is also crucial. This is like a reset for your brain, which will not only reduce stress but improve focus when working on individual tasks. And finally, it is always beneficial to receive support. Speaking with a friend, family member, therapist, or coworker can always take a lot of pressure off.

Now that some means of dealing with stress in the workplace have been discussed, we can get to improving relationships with coworkers.

The role of coworkers in the average American's normal life has changed dramatically throughout recent years. A coworker used to be a much more formal acquaintance to the average worker. Today, however, many spend more time with their coworkers than they do with their friends and family. The search for more meaningful work has many things that come with it, among these is the added emphasis on having a strong team behind your back and the desire to be a strong team member. Neither of these two is possible when getting along with your coworkers becomes difficult. Having good relationships with your coworkers is also important in career development. Getting better job opportunities can, like most things, often come down to winning a popularity contest.

There are many different means of securing good relationships that differ widely with time and circumstance. A few will be listed below:

Keep it simple

When starting at a new company, it can often be beneficial to meet with all your new coworkers one by one and informally. First impressions speak volumes, so taking an initiative in greeting others can help you in the relationships you establish in the long run. This process can also make the orientation process a lot easier for the more shy among us.

Humility and gratitude

People do not typically appreciate working with arrogant people, or people who aren't open to criticism. These attitudes will make it much harder to make friends, and people will generally try to avoid working with others who project these ugly traits. It is always important that you let your coworkers know that you are open and receptive to criticism and new ideas and it is also important that you avoid stepping on their toes with an arrogant attitude. Thanking people for their work and helping them along the way will also make people more agreeable to you.

Listen and observe actively

In the average workplace, as in anywhere else, it is usually a good idea to gain an understanding of the culture that surrounds you and its norms before criticising it. If you want to keep a good standing with your coworkers and bosses, it is important to show respect for the company and those who work for it. This will not only help you but others around you when they invariably try to emulate your performance, creating a better overall work environment.

Transparency and honesty

It is impossible to work with others without conflict. Not only is avoiding this conflict unsustainable, but it also hinders development. What is always more important is that you are able to deal with conflict productively and maturely whenever it arises. Under these circumstances, it becomes important to take responsibility and to avoid carrying blame too far. You should also never neglect to apologize when it is necessary.

Keep a clear expectation of the work relationship

Goals are usually more easily reached when sought after with planning to an end in mind. You do not have to turn communication with coworkers into some type of Machiavellian mind game, but you should be precise in what you say to others and keep preformed goals in mind when speaking with coworkers at times. This tip is especially useful for managers and bosses. Give the people below you a clear example of what the company wants from them and try to make your demands accessible yet practical. The more clarity that is provided to workers, the more confidence those workers will typically have when meeting the demands placed on them. Workers at all levels should avoid ambiguity when discussing work-related issues with others. It is important to remain objective and practical when discussing these matters, and any other attitude will generally be met with confusion and frustration.

Encourage and engage

Employees work best on a diet of praise and recognition about every two weeks. It is normal to desire being seen through your work and for your work to be acknowledged. It is not just a weightless platitude to assert that praise and recognition carry further among employees than do salaries and benefits, it is the truth. As Maya Angelou said, "people will forget what you said, people will forget what you did, but people will never forget how you made them feel." If you make people feel inferior, lazy, or useless, they are going to remember that you did that. If you make them feel valued, competent, and important, they are likewise going to remember that you did that.

Remember that coworkers are only humans

The expectations that you should place on your coworkers should always be grounded in reality, and erring on the side of minimalism. You only have the right to expect from coworkers about as much as you have to offer, whether that be a lot or a little. Try to always remember that your coworkers, whoever they might be, are just as human as you are. With that being said, it becomes important to come to know the people working around you. You should try to come to know what interests, hobbies, personal lives, dreams, and aspirations they have. Allow them their privacy, but show them that you take a personal interest in their happenings. The more that you do this, the stronger bonds and relationships you will develop. Getting to know who works around you can make not only your work life but also your own inner life all the more meaningful.

Embrace differences between individuals

It is easy to underestimate the difficulty in getting to know new coworkers. It can be very intimidating or even frustrating to go through this process, especially with coworkers who can be disagreeable or tyrannical. These are normal issues to confront though, and ones that never go away. Knowing how to deal with these people and situations can be tricky, as there are no manuals or textbooks that teach how to, but erring on the side of professional courtesy is a must. Seeing the people you work with more as humans and less as coworkers is always beneficial in supporting strong relationships. As humans, those who you work with are bound to differ from you in a wide variety of ways. Always be respectful of those differences, as they are usually good things for you to be around. Also, in modernity, it is important to remain cognizant of your own conduct at every moment of a workday.

Develop your people skills

As you already know, good relationships start with good people skills. These are otherwise known as "soft skills." Some examples of soft skills that are advantageous to have in the workforce are leadership skills, proclivity toward teamwork, problem-solving skills, communication skills, flexibility/adaptability, work ethic, and interpersonal skills. All of these skills have one common theme: sociability. Without being sociable with your coworkers, you can never expect to build and maintain good relationships with them, nor can you expect to build and maintain your career. If you are not sociable, then you may remain at the bottom of every work hierarchy that you find yourself in, or you may not even be able to keep work.

Identify your relationship needs

This one is closely related to the one on keeping a clear expectation of the work relationship, but it is also important to be clear with yourself and others about what you need to work properly. It is not fair to let yourself get bullied into relationships and situations that do not work in your favor. You have a right and an obligation to serve your own best interest, and this can be done effectively without making other people around you suffer. The first step in doing this, however, is specifying your needs. This is most easily done by journaling on what bothers you and brainstorming methods of fixing the issues at hand. Once skills in doing this are developed, they can be applied to any and all facets of your life, it just takes the initiative to get this ball rolling.

Schedule times to build relationships

Scheduling a time period is one of the best things that you can do for yourself in the contemporary world. This is also true for building relationships. Even if the time each day is minuscule, 5 to 20 minutes, for example, over time this practice can and will help to improve the relationships with your coworkers.

Appreciate your coworkers

If there is one thing that everyone who you ever work with is always going to want, it is an appreciation for the work that they do. If you keep in mind that everyone else is doing more or less as much as you are doing then appreciating them becomes much easier. Showing that you are thankful for the work that others have to offer will invariably open the door to better relationships and even boosted company morale.

Positivity is important

Focusing on remaining positive will not only help you with your mood and well-being, but it will also help those around you. Positivity is a trait that is attractive and contagious, and it makes working (and living) much easier and enjoyable. Negativity, on the other hand, is repellent and leads only to further suffering. Remaining positive not only improves your relationships with your coworkers, but it also boasts many health benefits, including lowered heart rate and blood pressure, a strengthened immune system, lower levels of cortisol and blood clotting, less muscle strain and heartburn, lower levels of chronic pain and disease, and even a longer average lifespan. With all things considered, a person really can't even afford negativity.

Controlling and managing boundaries

Managing boundaries becomes important when there are uneven distributions of time and energy being spent on the people and things that you work with. For example, if one coworker of yours wants to speak with you for hours out of every day while another never speaks to you, it could be a good idea to close that gap. While working, it is never a pleasant feeling to be spread thin. Meanwhile, it is ill-advised to neglect to keep enough on your plate. To maintain balance boundaries sometimes need to be set. It is important to be assertive while doing this also. If you cannot afford certain social interactions, then there is no shame in turning them down politely.

Gossip is a destructive force

The biggest killer of workplace companionship is usually gossip. This is also the most cowardly means of getting your points across, and it should be avoided at all costs. When an issue with a coworker arises, it is always important to address it directly with the coworker in question and usually no one else. Playing office politics often ends badly for all parties involved and seldom gets any problems solved.

Active listening

When a person speaks, they want reassurance that they are going to be listened to. If they are not listened to, then there is no reason why they should speak and, just like that, a coworker becomes ostracized and alienated. This is why it is important to listen actively to what a coworker says and to absorb the contents with an open mind. If you do this, people will be more inclined to trust you, and you will become more admired at your place of work.

Improving workplace relationships can be one of the most difficult aspects of keeping a job but, if done effectively, it can make working much easier and more enjoyable. It can be pretty surprising to see just how quickly things in a workplace can plunge into chaos if these steps, or others like them, are never taken by anyone. Once plans for improving relationships are administered within a workplace, however, the whole of the company improves, yourself included.

Chapter Two: Controlling Emotions

The workplace can be one of the most difficult places to control emotions in. No matter how hard you try, those difficult days are always bound to come up. In your personal life, your reactions to stressful situations are much more free, but in the workplace, your reactions are subject to the scrutiny of your coworkers. Any emotional outbursts while working can not only damage your professional reputation and productivity, but they can even get you fired.

Under normal circumstances, it is usually easy to maintain composure in the workplace, but under more stressful circumstances, such as staff layoffs, budget cuts, and department changes, staying calm can prove difficult, if not impossible. Under these circumstances, however, it becomes even more important to keep your temper, as bosses typically consider the demeanor of their employees when deciding who gets laid off. You have complete freedom on how you react to certain situations, but that freedom comes with responsibility, especially in the workplace.

It may seem easy to decide how you're going to react in certain situations with hindsight, but it is always advisable to explore techniques in dealing with these situations and emotions. Here, we will discuss many negative emotions associated with employment, as well as many methods of coping with these emotions.

The most commonly reported negative emotions among workers are as follows:

Worry/nervousness, frustration/irritation, dislike, anger/aggravation, disappointment/unhappiness

And now we will get into some strategies in dealing with these unhealthy emotions.

Worry/nervousness

These are two of the most unpleasant and unhealthy emotions on the spectrum, and, unfortunately for workers, these two emotions plague virtually every workplace. This anxiety can stem from a number of sources: fear of getting laid off, social problems, low salaries, large workload, and so on, and be compounded with problems at home, or with family or friends. A small amount of stress can be a productive thing, but once it becomes chronic anxiety, health problems start to occur. Here are some tips on how to avoid excessive anxiety:

Break cycles of worry

Do not surround yourself with anxiety. If you can foresee needless anxiety stemming from a situation or a conversation, avoid that anxiety. Try to minimize the number of anxiety inducing things that you have to deal with.

Try deep breathing exercises

These help primarily to slow down your breathing and heart rate. There are all sorts of different deep breathing exercises that you can learn about on the internet. For one, there is cyclical breathing, breathe for 4 seconds followed by holding for 4 seconds, and then out breaths for 4 seconds followed by holding for 4 seconds. When doing these exercises, it is important to focus on your breathing and nothing else. In addition to these exercises, there are other physical relaxation exercises that will help reduce workplace stress, including progressive muscle relaxation.

Focus on improving the situation

Whatever it is worrying you in regards to work, brainstorming solutions and making attempts at them will help reduce your anxiety. Doing these things will also make you a more valuable asset to your company.

Journal your worries down

Simply writing down the things that bother you will do a lot to alleviate the anxiety surrounding them. This technique also helps to curtail sleep problems and nightmares, as worries that we write down during the day don't typically bother us by night. Once these are written down, you can then schedule times to deal with these issues. Before that time comes, let these issues leave you and go about your day. When that time comes, make sure to perform a proper risk analysis before putting any plans into place.

Worry and nervousness can decrease self-confidence and lead to health complications. it is always important to trail these negative emotions away and remain confident and secure.

Frustration/irritation

Frustration is more often than not caused by the feeling of being trapped or stuck at a point that you want to get out of, but cannot. This feeling can be caused by a number of things, especially at work. A colleague blocking a project of yours, a boss too disorganized to catch a meeting on time, or a phone call held out longer than necessary are just a few examples that come to mind. Frustration, whatever its causes, should always be dealt with quickly because when it is not, it can accumulate into anger and other even more negative emotions.

There are, however, many ways of dealing with this awful emotion, a few of which are listed below:

Stopping to evaluate

The best thing to do when feelings of frustration arise is to stop what you are doing and take the time to evaluate them. Writing your frustrations down in this stage can help. After this is done, think of some positive aspects of your current situation. This will improve your mood and reduce further frustration.

Look for positive things

Again, finding silver linings in a frustrating situation will make you see the events unfolding in a new light. This change in your thinking will improve your mood, among other things. If it is a person who is causing you frustration, then keep in mind that it is probably not personal, and if it is an event or situation, then it can probably be solved. Try to move on from this step as much as possible.

Recall the last time you felt frustrated

If you can remember the last thing that you were frustrated about, then you can probably remember how that thing eventually resolved itself. Looking at things with hindsight, they always work out fine. You can also probably recall that your feelings of frustration did not do much to help you in that last situation, so to assume that they are helping you this time around would not be very prudent. Perspective is everything, and so many issues lose so much of their stature when seen from different angles.

Dislike

Dislike for certain coworkers is inevitable, and when it pops up, it seldom goes away. We all have to work with people who we dislike at one point or another, so when these people arrive, it is important to take steps toward dealing with them responsibly. Some of the best things that you can do in these situations are to:

Show respect

You are never obligated to get along with everyone you work with, but you are, in many ways, obligated to show them all respect. When these situations arise, pride and ego are two things which you should set aside, even if the other party(s) are not willing to. This will allow you to come out of the experience with your dignity intact, whatever the outcomes may be.

Be assertive

If a coworker is rude or unprofessional to you, do not be afraid to tell them so. If you do so with certainty and fairness, they might be inclined to change some of their attitudes and behaviors in the future.

Anger/aggravation

Anger is arguably the most destructive emotion contained in a human. This is especially true when the anger is out of control in the workplace. It is also an emotion which most of us do not handle very well. As far as work is concerned, there is typically very little room for anger, which is problematic because much of it then gets taken home with us. Controlling this emotion is one of the most important steps in keeping any given job, especially for those who have difficulties with this. Some tips for dealing with this emotion are listed below:

Watch for the early signs of anger

No one else can detect when your anger is building up quite like you can, so detecting it early is your own responsibility. As was mentioned before, you decide how to react to situations, so if you react in anger, no one holds accountability for that happening.

When anger arises, take a break from what you are doing. When you start to get angry, closing your eyes and trying the aforementioned deep breathing exercises can help you hugely. These actions will do a lot to interrupt your angry thoughts and help to put your mind back on a more positive, relaxed pathway, reducing irrational statements and decisions made.

Picture yourself when you get angry

Imagining how you look and behave will usually give you some well-needed perspective on the situation at hand. For example, if you have the urge to shout at a coworker, think about what you would look like doing so: flustered, mean, and demanding. With that imagery in mind, it is easy to see that you would not be a good coworker in making that decision.

Disappointment/unhappiness

Disappointment and unhappiness are two of the more pullulated emotions in modern workplaces. These two are almost equal to anger in their unhealthiness; in fact, unhappiness may be unhealthier. These can also have detrimental impacts on your productivity, as they can leave you feeling exhausted and drained, and also less inclined to take risks in the future. Here are some steps that can be taken to curtail the effects of these awful emotions.

Consider your mindset

Try to always keep in mind that things will not always go your way. If they did, then life would become prosaic and meaningless. It is, sometimes, the adversity and the suffering that give life its meat. Do not try to avoid these things, the answer to these problems lies in the willingness to confront them.

Set and adjust your goals

Disappointment can often stem from neglecting to reach a goal. This rarely means, however, that the goal is no longer reachable. It is natural to feel disappointment in these situations, but you must always find the willpower to pick yourself back up. You could, for example, keep your goal, but just make a small change. Anything that will help you to get past the disappointments that you face.

Record your thoughts

One method for dealing with negative emotions is to write them down. When you feel unhappy or disappointed, try writing down what is bothering you, and be specific about your concerns. Is it your job that is bothering you? A coworker? Do you have too heavy of a workload? Writing these concerns down will help you to single out what exactly is bothering you and how you can improve on these areas of concern. Remember that you always have more powers than you think in improving a situation.

Remember to smile

Forcing a smile onto your face can actually make you feel happier and relieve stress. In addition, this activity also releases the neurotransmitters dopamine, endorphins, and serotonin, which all lower heart rate and blood pressure. The endorphins released also act as natural painkillers, and the serotonin acts as a natural antidepressant. Smiling will also make you look more attractive to those around you, further bettering the relationships you have with your coworkers.

Now that the main emotions that have adverse effects on most workers have been covered, let's take a look at some more strategies for dealing with these:

Compartmentalize your stressors

Try to keep stress and baggage from work and home in those respective places. You can use mental techniques, such as imagining the stressors locked away in a box for the time being. If you do not try to compartmentalize these issues, then waters will get very muddied up in your personal life, and things will become very complicated.

Identify your own self-talk

Relay to yourself what you tell yourself. By doing this, you may find yourself repeating thoughts and phrases to yourself that are not necessarily true or helpful. Try to identify your own thoughts that may be misleading or based on thinking errors. Doing this will help you move on from some of your worse points and attitudes into a more productive and expansive mindset.

Identify and accept your emotion

There is virtually nothing you can do to control an emotion that you are not even willing to come to terms with having. It is like denying the existence of a spider right in front of your eyes, the spider will just get bigger and bigger until it is all that you can see. In identifying what emotion(s) you are having and accepting that they are a natural part of life, you are taking lots of power away from them. In doing this, you are also becoming a greater solver of your own problems.

Affirm your rights

There are many places in life, work especially, where you are bound to feel like you have no rights and no control over what happens to you. By identifying your rights and your powers, you are giving yourself some perspective on the things that are in and out of your control. After taking some time to do this, you may find that you are much more powerful than you think you are. This will improve your mood and your self-confidence to affirm these rights that you have.

Communicate strategically

Anyone can drone on about the things that they do not like, but it takes skill and grit to actually get things done to fix all their problems. When you are trying to communicate with others, especially disagreements, it is always important to be precise in your language. This will allow you to communicate your qualms more effectively, and it will also decrease the chance of having misunderstandings and heated arguments. When trying to get a point across, try to come into the situation with some idea of what you want to get accomplished and your probability of having a productive conversation will increase dramatically. If others reply emotionally, let them vent and be understanding. You may learn more from them than they will from you. Ask for more details as well, and the two of you will probably come closer to an understanding because of it.

Be objective

Try to look at whatever is bothering you from both analytic and synthetic approaches. An analytic approach will help you understand the one issue with more depth and clarity, while a synthetic approach will help you understand the issue within the class of all of your possible issues. It is important to look into things with depth and focus, but seeing things as parts of your whole understanding will help you to make connections and find out why these certain things bother you through free associations.

Emotions are never right or wrong, they are only felt. There is no shame in feeling emotions unless of course, the emotion is shame. Emotions will always come and go and are always wiser than the ego. Each one of us, however, has free will in how we react to life's vicissitudes. Controlling emotions is not always easy; in fact, sometimes it becomes nearly impossible. But this skill is just like any other in that it can be improved with practice and diligence.

Chapter Three: Building Confidence and Finding Long-Lasting Success

Low self-esteem is one of the most detrimental traits a person can have to overall well-being. One of the trickiest things about this trait is that it can be very deeply rooted in negative childhood experiences and then compounded by more negative experiences later in adulthood, such as ill-health, getting a divorce, losing a job, toxic relationships, or a general sense of having no control.

Low self-esteem can also increase the likelihood of developing mental health disorders and the severity of their effects. This trait has a complex and often comorbid relationship with disorders such as borderline personality disorder and depression. In depression, for instance, the disorder of depression can lead to a lowering of self-esteem, which in turn can lead to more depression. This is a destructive personality trait that can work with so many other factors to damage and destroy you.

Those who suffer from low self-esteem often view the world as a very hostile and unwelcoming place and themselves as its victim. This is not a great worldview to take, as people who see the world in this way are often reluctant to assert and express themselves. They then miss out on valuable opportunities and experiences that they otherwise would have had, feeling powerless to live life to its fullest. This creates yet another systemic loop of missing out on life, followed by feeling more and more inferior. It is easy to get caught up on this, but sometimes very hard to get out of it.

Here are some tips and techniques on how to build your confidence and avoid the systems of self-degradation that low self-esteem can cause:

Make two lists: one listing your achievements, and one listing your strengths

It may be beneficial to include a second party in this process, as low self-esteem can morph our self-perceptions to a point at which it becomes impossible to be objective when qualifying ourselves. Doing this will immediately make you feel more confident and ready to take on the day's challenges. It will also give you some perspective on where your personal development is at. This is a great means of boosting self-esteem and finding out what traits you possess that you can use to your advantage in the future.

Look at yourself in a more positive light

You have intrinsic value. You are a unique person, and there is something sovereign about you. You are the architect of your life, you build its foundations and choose its contents. It is important to remind yourself of these things throughout life. Looking at yourself through a positive light is the only way you can afford to look at yourself, and it makes life so much easier. When negative thoughts such as "I am a loser" or "no one wants me around" come to mind, it is your responsibility to identify and challenge those thoughts. Treat yourself like someone who deserves to be purged of thoughts like those, because they never help you.

Pay more attention to your personal hygiene

Take regular showers, brush your teeth, clip your nails and so on. Outside appearances are known to affect self-concept.

Wear only clean clothes that make you feel confident

Try wearing the clothes that you think you and the others around you will like the best. Consider throwing out some of your old, worn-out clothes for newer, better clothes.

Eat good foods as part of a healthier, more balanced diet

The benefits of doing this are innumerable. This tip should be followed above all others listed here. You should also make mealtime an especially mindful and relaxing time, taking time to enjoy every moment. This is also the time of the day when your senses are most active.

Exercise regularly

This is another incredibly important tip. Set some time away each day, say 20 to 30 minutes, for a brisk walk or a bike ride. In addition, it could help to set aside time 3 to 4 times a week for more vigorous forms of exercise. These could be weight lifting, team sports, martial arts, and so on. This will not only increase your self-esteem, but it will also reduce your risk of chronic disease, increase your energy levels, and even improve the functioning of your brain.

Get enough sleep at night

This is a big factor in living a healthy life that all too often gets ignored by modern people. Getting an appropriate amount of sleep each night (7 to 9 hours) can not only boost your mood and your self-esteem, but it can also reduce your risk of developing heart disease and/or high blood pressure. Doing this also makes your waking life more enjoyable and productive.

Reduce levels of stress

There are many different means of doing this. Deep breathing exercises, exercise, and venting to others come to mind. This will increase your confidence because, in part, of all the things that you will accomplish, you will increase your energy.

Make your living space clean, neat, comfortable, and attractive

Seeing clutter, dirt, and general disorganization activates the same neural pathways that seeing predators like snakes and spiders activates. You also feel about the same in the two instances, flustered and uncomfortable. This is why it is wise to keep your living space tidy, to clear up your mind if nothing else.

Do the things that you enjoy doing more often

This one may be obvious, but taking part in activities that you enjoy will make you much more fulfilled and confident. You can get all of your work done and fulfill all of your obligations in a day and still be able to do the things that you enjoy doing if you are persistent.

Pursue artistic endeavors

Painting, practicing an instrument, writing, dancing, whatever artistic activity you prefer will help to boost your confidence and happiness. It will also reduce your levels of stress. You might even find that you have artistic talents the likes of which you were not aware of. You never know until you try.

Set challenges for yourself that you can realistically meet

Setting goals that are out of your league can be a good way to boost productivity, but they also may reduce your self-esteem if you always expect to meet them. It is advisable to be realistic with yourself when setting your own personal goals. If you are, then you won't feel stretched thin, and you will be able to meet your own expectations more easily.

Get started on some of the things that you have been putting off

Finishing the tasks that you procrastinate on is always a great way to relieve stress and anxiety. It leaves you with free time afterward to relax and unwind. This will also boost your confidence by showing you your own competence and work ethic.

Be nice to people, and do things for them

Being altruistic will not only give you the immediate feeling of joy, but it will also make others appreciate you more, in turn making you even more confident. You will gain the respect of others as well as additional self-respect by behaving in this manner.

All these tips mentioned above should help to boost your self-esteem. This trait is, however, always going to be a work in progress for those of us who have low self-esteem. This is why it is important to stay persistent in fending off these sometimes die hard self-debasing traits and attitudes. Once some confidence has been found, however, it becomes beneficial to know what to do with it. How do you become successful with your new attitude, and how do you maintain that success? Hopefully, these next few tips will help you to answer those questions.

Aim big

This one is thrown around a lot but very rarely adhered to. Michelangelo, a centuries-old ideogram of success, once said that "the greater danger for most of us lies not in setting our aim too high and falling short, but in setting our aim too low, and achieving our mark." This quote holds especially true when imagining if Michelangelo had never become an artist, taking instead a "normal" day job. It is hard to tell where art would be today as a result.

Here we have the idea of hefty goals never being met as preferable to small goals successfully achieved. This is obviously not always the appropriate strategy in goal setting, but as we get older, we tend to lose energy and get a bit more lackluster in our goals and operations. Keeping your ambition is like keeping your youth, you get to retain so much of your potential and energy. So many people place realism over their aspirations, which is fine for them, but it should be noted that there is room for the both of them despite your age or walk in life.

Find what it is that you love to do most and do it

Media mogul Oprah Winfrey once said "you know you are on the road to success if you would do your job, and not be paid for it." This is a great one to consider while at work. If you can imagine yourself being as successful as possible at your current job, you can probably see yourself spending most of your time doing this. If this happens to be a job that you hate doing, then this would mean only spending all your time doing things that you do not enjoy. There is no sense in living like this, so why not instead spend most of your time doing something that you love to do?

If you take this step and success did not meet you, then you still spent all your time doing the things you love to do the most. You also probably learned a lot and developed lots of skills surrounding whatever these activities are. Many people do the things that they love to do most on the side for years, just for the sake of doing those things.

Learn how to balance life well

Phil Knight, the CEO of Nike Inc., once said "there is an immutable conflict at work in life and in business, a constant battle between peace and chaos. Neither can be mastered, but both can be influenced. How you go about that is the key to success." Those who strive greatly for success often make the mistake of placing the object of their success at the center of their lives. While it is important to work hard and to stay on top of your obligations, it is more important to lead an enjoyable life.

Workers tend to think that their job, whatever it may be, may lead them to success if they just work harder. They often work for long hours late into their evenings each day to make success happen. This is ill-advised, however, because whatever gains that come out of it come at the costs of their health, rest, and even their lives being enjoyable. This type of lifestyle burns people out and often makes them resentful as a result. To add to that, the successes that they do gain are usually only marginal. This lifestyle also destroys a worker's personal and social life. It leaves no time to go out with friends and little time to work on personal projects. Maintaining a balance between work and social life is one of the hallmarks of success that needs to be managed carefully and persistently.

Lose your fear of failure

Henry Ford, the founder of Ford motors, once said "failure is simply the opportunity to begin again, this time more intelligently." There is an anecdote of yet another important figure of the industrial revolution in respect to this tip; it took Thomas Edison several hundred failed attempts before he created the first successful light bulb. Afterward, one interviewer asked him "how do you feel after all of your failed attempts?" His response was tactful and wise: "I did not fail, I learned hundreds of ways *not* to invent the lightbulb."

From each and every one of his "failures," he took away a lesson of some sort. From these, he gained perspective on what would and would not work. He used a good attitude and an eye for finding helpful experiences to lead to his eventual success. This is the way that anyone who strives for success must conduct themselves.

The moral of the Thomas Edison story could be to monitor and learn from your own failures and turn them into valuable learning experiences. These will give you better ideas on how and how not to go about your work. You will also learn a lot about the work itself.

Keep your resolution to succeed unwaveringly

Colonel Sanders, the founder of KFC, was once quoted as saying "I made a resolve then that I was going to amount to something if I could. And no hours, nor amount of labor, nor the amount of money would deter me from giving the best that there was in me. And I have done that ever since, and I win by it. I know."

This tip is incredibly important, and it can be used in tandem with the one listed below very effectively. Giving up on your goals after a failure is the easiest thing in the world to do. If the failure is large and devastating enough, it can even seem like the only option. It takes, however, a burning and inextinguishable desire to succeed to curtail these defeatist urges though.

You have to put 100% into the things you go into, or else your plans will always fall through. If you do not give your goals everything that you have then each failure and each setback is going to hurt and dissuade you even more than the last. This will continue until you push back and fight for your dreams with everything that you have.

Success, in whatever form, is a hard thing to achieve. If it were easy to achieve, then everyone would be successful, but it instead discriminates against those who do not work for it. It is not possible to find success without grit and sacrifice, a point which brings us to our last tip on finding long-lasting success.

Be a person of action

Leonardo Da Vinci, one of the greatest geniuses of all time, once observed "it had long since come to my attention that people of accomplishment rarely sat back and let things happen to them. They went out and happened to things." This one will not only lead you to success, but it will also lead you to be mean and to be proud. The world is not kept running by people waiting for things to just happen to them, it is kept running by industrious people taking charge of themselves and the responsibilities they keep. It is useless to sit around and expect magic beans. It is almost always useful, however, to get to work on making your aspirations realities.

The tips and techniques mentioned above should help to bolster your self-esteem and make you more successful. If these goals are important to you, try applying these techniques in your everyday life and see if they work for you.

Chapter Four: Social Engineering and Leadership

The importance of social engineering and leadership are often underestimated by contemporary thinkers. Most people are so absorbed in manipulating and taking down hierarchical structures that they neglect to figure out how to manifest themselves within these structures. Whether you have a proclivity toward leadership or not, it still remains important to have a working knowledge of leadership and how it works among groups of people.

Leaders, above all else, help themselves and others in making steps toward doing the right things. In doing this, they build an inspiring vision, set direction, and create new possibilities. Leadership is, in part, about mapping out the route to your team's successful future. It is challenging, but also exciting, dynamic, and inspiring. Setting the direction of the pack is not the only responsibility of a leader though. They are also obligated to guide their people in these directions in a smooth and efficient way. This may be the more challenging skill which takes more time to develop.

This chapter and its tips on the process of leadership will be based on the "transformational model" of leadership proposed by James MacGregor Burns and further developed by Bernard Bass. This model more so focuses on bringing about change through visionary leadership than the normative managerial processes designed to maintain the current performance of given groups.

An overview of leadership

The following are a few traits of an effective leader:

1. Succeeds in creating an inspiring vision of the future
2. Inspires and motivates people to engage with that vision
3. Manages the delivery of the vision
4. Builds and coaches a team, so that it becomes more effective in meeting the vision

Effective leadership requires all of these traits working together with one another. Next, it would be helpful to explore each one of these elements in greater detail.

Succeeds in creating an inspiring vision of the future

In the workforce, a vision that a boss prognosticates needs to be a convincing, realistic, and attractive depiction of the situation that you want to be in in the future. This vision should set priorities, and provide direction and a marker to people to assure that all are able to see whether or not the goals set forth have been achieved.

To create a reliable vision, leaders must first assess and analyze their current situation to get an understanding of where to go. Some steps that are appropriate to take in this stage are considering the evolution of their industry in the future, considering the behaviors of their competitors, and how to innovate successfully to shape their business for competition in the future marketplace. The next step is to undergo some scenario analysis to assess the validity of their vision.

Leadership is, therefore, proactive rather than reactive; looking ahead, problem-solving, and constantly evolving.

Once a leader's vision has been developed, it is necessary to sell the vision. To do this, they have to make the vision compelling and convincing. A compelling vision allows people to understand, embrace, see, and feel it. Effective leaders can communicate their visions effectively and clearly. They are able to speak about their visions in ways that people can relate to, and they inform people in an inspired way. This makes people more receptive to their ideas and more inclined to follow what they have to say.

Shared values and vision creation are two major components of leadership. Those who can develop skills in these two areas are more likely to succeed in leadership roles.

Inspires and motivates people to engage with that vision

The foundation of leadership is a compelling vision. This vision is only met, however, by a leader's ability to inspire and motivate their followers. At the beginning of most projects, it is easier to stay enthusiastic, which in turn makes it easier to win support for it than in other stages of the project. Afterward, the initial enthusiasm fades is when it becomes more difficult to maintain an inspiring vision moving forward. People change along with their attitudes and working methods, as well as their goals. Good leadership requires recognizing this phenomenon and working hard throughout a given project to be cognizant of others' needs, hopes, and desires while meeting the vision at hand. It is a juggling act of altruism and pragmatism that helps wherever it goes.

One means of linking effort, motivation, and outcome is known as expectancy theory. This place is an emphasis on leaders linking two main expectations that their followers have. These are listed below:

- The expectation of hard work leading to good results.
- The expectation of good results leading to incentives or rewards.

People with these expectations foresee both intrinsic and extrinsic rewards and therefore work harder to achieve success.

One other approach includes repeatedly restating the vision with added emphasis on its rewards and communicating the vision in a more effective and attractive way.

Expert power is one of the most helpful things that a leader can have. People are more inclined to admire and believe in leaders with this because they are seen as experts at what they do. Expertise comes with credibility, respect, and prestige. This also potentially gives people a right and even an obligation to lead others. Having and displaying competence gives leaders a much easier time motivating and inspiring their followers.

Natural charisma and appeal can also serve as conduits for a leader's motivation of and influence over people, as well as other sources of power. These other sources of power include the ability to assign tasks to people and to pay bonuses.

Managing the delivery of the vision

This area of leadership applies more to management than any of these other tips.

Leaders always need to make sure that they are properly managing the work necessary for delivering their vision. This can be done by either themselves, a manager, or a team of managers delegated by the leader to deliver the vision of the leader.

To achieve this, team members need to meet their performance goals linked to the company's vision. Some means of seeing that this is done are KPIs (key performance indicators), performance management, and project management. One other way of ensuring that the vision is being met is a management style called management by wandering around (MBWA). This style ensures that all the steps that need to be taken are taken in meeting any given goals.

Another trait of an effective leader is the ability to manage change well. Leadership is, after all, constant evolution and adjusting to work's vicissitudes. Managing changes smoothly and efficiently ensures that all goals will be met and obstacles overcome throughout the course of realizing the leader's vision. This can only be done, however, with the backing and support of the people behind the leader.

Building and coaching a team to achieve the vision

Some of the more crucial activities carried out by transformational leaders are individual and team development. Without these, there would be nothing for the leader to lead. The first step in developing a team that a leader has to take is to come to understand team dynamics. There are several popular and well-established models that can describe these to a leader, including

Belbin's team roles approach, and the forming, storming, norming, performing, and adjourning theory of Bruce Tuckman. A more in-depth analysis of this theory is featured below.

Forming

The forming step involves a team coming together at the beginning of a venture to figure out the goals of the group out and how to go about accomplishing these. Members tend to be impersonal and polite during this period as everyone is still getting oriented within the team.

Storming

The storming phase is a bit more selective and critical. In this phase, the leadership may be questioned along with group members ideas. This is very much a culling-off phase of the process as many of the group's members will feel overwhelmed and disconcerted by the turbulence and criticism. Some of them who do not leave after this stage give up on the goal at hand as well. And some just simply do not want to do what is asked of them.

Norming

Norming is the step at which the group comes together to agree on a singular plan for achieving the common goal. In this stage, members of the group are encouraged to yield their ideas for the betterment of the group, and they also come to know and understand each other better, building stronger relationships. It is the working toward a common goal that brings the team members together.

Performing

By the performing stage of the process, the group members are able to work toward accomplishing the goal without very much outside supervision or input. They also come to understand each other's needs better and how to work with one another to accomplish the goal at hand.

Adjourning

In the adjourning stage, the opportunity to reflect on unsuccessful and successful outcomes comes about. Members of the group can use these outcomes to gauge what they should do when working on future tasks. This will help smooth out the process of meeting a goal in the future.

The next time you find yourself working in a group on a certain task, monitor the group's progress through these stages. Group members tend to move through these stages in all sorts of different orders. They actually rarely happen in the order listed above. If, however, team members are aware of the steps that they are moving through—which they usually are not—then they can typically work through these steps much more efficiently and effectively. Walking yourself through these steps listed above will help you navigate the happenings of your workplace better in the future.

Leadership

A competent leader always does their best to ensure that team members are equipped with all the abilities and skills necessary to do their jobs and achieve the overarching vision. To do this, it is necessary to give and receive feedback on a day-to-day basis, as well as to train and coach team members on a regular basis as well. These steps will improve individual and team performances dramatically.

Good leaders lead, but great leaders lead and find leadership potential. When leading a team, it is always helpful to find leadership abilities in others, whatever their current positions may be. This paves the way for not only differentiation in hierarchical status, but also for further development beyond the leader's influence or even stay. It can also give a leader a surprisingly helpful example in other competent workers.

The terms "leader" and "leadership" are often misused to describe people who are actually in managerial positions. These people are often highly skilled and have great work-ethics, but that does not necessarily make them great leaders.

Workplaces are all too often hoisted up on people who others consider to be leaders but are actually managers. These managers often do not provide any aspirations or even long-term goals for their team members, which is fine in the short term, but eventually leads to feelings of meaninglessness and even resentment.

The next discussion points that should be delved into would have to be group dynamics and social engineering. These are important realms to know about when entering a new workplace, or any given social setting for that matter. Here we will look into what group dynamics are and what you need to know about them to master them.

Group dynamics

Group dynamics, whether ignored by participants or not, play a major role in any culture, organization, or unit. People with differing ideas and perspectives make these groups up. It is very rare that all people and their ideologies are homogeneous within any given group. It is, in fact, also dangerous. Leaders are looked up to within these groups maintain the unity of purpose and cohesiveness of the unit. The cultural bonds within these units must be developed more at certain times than in others. Once these bonds are developed, the further effort has to be put in to nurture them.

Dysfunction within these groups occurs with alienation among specific members. When a member feels ostracized, there is very little keeping them from acting out in unpredictable ways. This is bound to come up at times and when it does, the leader can struggle to remain objective as the structure of the cohesive unit starts to fall apart. These are usually the worst periods of chaos in the histories of groups. It is these periods, however, that separate good leaders from bad ones.

At all times, if they are understandable or appropriate, the leader or manager must continue to recognize the team member causing the disturbance as an integral part of the group. Further alienation typically leads only to further disturbance. At these times, it would be beneficial for the leader to look at the employee causing the disturbance as being a special employee, one who could use the leader's help or skills, one who remains part of the group, and even one who may be there to teach the leader something. A review of the nature of the communication, power, and corporate climate of the unit would also be beneficial under these circumstances to further understand the team member's point of view and avoid further disturbances in the future.

A leader must also have abilities in objective introspection. It is not advisable or even possible to guide or help others unless these skills are developed. It is putting the cart before the horse. A leader recognizing their own insecurities will be more easily able to perceive and recognize staff dysfunctions as being symptomatic of systematic dysfunctions. The ego will be more open to rationality once personal problems are more specifically addressed. It takes a secure and mature person to decide that their staff is ultimately more important than their own ideas, moving forward.

Once new steps are taken after dysfunctions, much progress can be made, and the company can often be left better off than they were beforehand because of this. The staff can find new means of communication and ways to relate to one another, they can find also find new modes of behavior all together that could even boost their self-esteem or overall well-being. Fortunately, for the leader, everyone at the company could then boast of having a manager with a plethora of newfound ideas and attitudes. All these intricacies and regulations tend to make working in a group very complicated at times, but if all of these steps are stuck to, and everyone pulls their own weight, the benefits of teamwork can be innumerable.

Conclusion

Thank you for making it through to the end of *Emotional Intelligence*. Let's hope it was informative and answered any questions you had previously regarding the subject. The purpose of this book was primarily to supply you with some tools for fostering your emotional intelligence. This is, however, a trait that takes lots of time and effort to improve on. The next steps for you would be to consider looking into any other resources on this subject and seeing if any are a good fit for you.

This book's subject was broad. Emotional intelligence is a wide concept with lots of components, which means that there is a lot of room for improvement. This book mostly covered emotional intelligence through a lens suitable for use in the workplace, but to truly gain skills in dealing with your emotions you have to live a lifestyle, of sorts, devoted to that goal, in and outside of work.

The workplace is a very important place to keep your emotions under control though. Attitudes and demeanors that are acceptable in most of the public arena just aren't in many workplaces. It is always ideal to separate your work life from your home life, of course, but it is even more ideal to keep a demeanor that is acceptable and respectable everywhere you go.

Finally, thank you again for finishing this book. Continue to apply the principles mentioned here in your life, and you are bound to see some positive changes.

Emotional Intelligence at Work

A Self-Help Guide That Teaches You to Build Your Social Skills and Establish Strong Relationships with Your Peers

By: Lawrence Franz

Introduction

Thank you for downloading *Emotional Intelligence.* Workplace stress is one of the worst health problems plaguing the modern world, accounting for 12.5 million work days lost in the United States alone as of 2016. Workplace stress also causes many physical and mental health problems. Among these are migraines, heightened blood pressure and heart rate, chronic anxiety, and paranoia, to name a few. Within the following chapters, we will go over some of the more useful methods of handling emotions within the workplace, and day-to-day life as well.

There are many facets of emotional intelligence that are extremely useful in the workplace that are often ignored. All too many people take new jobs, gain bad relationships with their coworkers, do not try to resolve their issues, and flee promptly. This hardly works in the short term and never works in the long term. If tools to handle emotions are never gained, then the same issues are always going to arise despite the workplace or living situation. If you have problems with working, then why not solve the problem at its source—your emotions?

This book will feature advice on a number of topics: improving interpersonal connections at work, controlling emotions, building confidence, finding long-lasting success, social engineering, and leadership. In all of these subjects, the reader should find at least one thing to take away from all this. Emotional intelligence is not something which should be underestimated. It can be one of the most important traits that a person can have or develop throughout life.

There are many great books on the market covering this subject. Thank you again for downloading this one. Enjoy!

Chapter One: Improving Interpersonal Connections at Work

A workplace can often be a demanding, high-stress environment to find oneself in. All this pressure can be amplified even higher when interpersonal connections are either not being made or are in bad conditions in the workplace. This is why it is of the utmost importance to improve the relationships one has with their coworkers and to keep improving on them continually. In this chapter, we will look at some useful tips and techniques for improving relationships with coworkers and working more effectively within group settings.

The first step in improving relationships with coworkers would have to be a check on your own workplace stressors. Before trying to fix what is going on with other workers, it is important to try to fix whatever is going on with you. To manage stress from the outward would be to hit the bullseye on the wrong target. Some of the most common workplace stressors that plague most modern employees are excessive workloads, low salaries, work that is not challenging or engaging, lack of opportunity for enhancement or growth, lack of social support, unclear performance expectations or conflicting demands, and lack of control over job-related decisions. Odds are that, if you are employed, one or more of these stressors apply to you. There is no shame in this, in fact, it is the norm, with around 65% of Americans citing their top source of stress as being work.

This epidemic of workplace stress is especially problematic because of its effects on the health and well-being of workers. Short-term stress is one thing, causing stomach aches, headaches, sleep disturbances, difficulty concentrating, and short temper. It is long-term stress, however, that causes the more dire effects, such as insomnia, anxiety, high blood pressure, and immune system weakening. This is where stress becomes very dangerous and potentially deadly. Most do not deal with their stress until it becomes a problem, but once it does, it may already be too late. This is why it is important to apply skills in coping with workplace stress.

One way of coping with workplace stress is to keep track of your stressors throughout the day. This can be done easily through journaling your inner thoughts throughout the day. Another way is to respond to stress in healthy ways. Rather than coping with unhealthy comfort foods, alcohol, or tobacco, you could try exercising, practicing one of your hobbies, or trying something new whenever you start to feel stressed out. Taking periods of rest is another important one that many neglect to do in these times, but effective working is just not possible without an occasional break. To work constantly is to build up a house on foundations of sand. Meditation is also crucial. This is like a reset for your brain, which will not only reduce stress but improve focus when working on individual tasks. And finally, it is always beneficial to receive support. Speaking with a friend, family member, therapist, or coworker can always take a lot of pressure off.

Now that some means of dealing with stress in the workplace have been discussed, we can get to improving relationships with coworkers.

The role of coworkers in the average American's normal life has changed dramatically throughout recent years. A coworker used to be a much more formal acquaintance to the average worker. Today, however, many spend more time with their coworkers than they do with their friends and family. The search for more meaningful work has many things that come with it, among these is the added emphasis on having a strong team behind your back and the desire to be a strong team member. Neither of these two is possible when getting along with your coworkers becomes difficult. Having good relationships with your coworkers is also important in career development. Getting better job opportunities can, like most things, often come down to winning a popularity contest.

There are many different means of securing good relationships that differ widely with time and circumstance. A few will be listed below:

Keep it simple

When starting at a new company, it can often be beneficial to meet with all your new coworkers one by one and informally. First impressions speak volumes, so taking an initiative in greeting others can help you in the relationships you establish in the long run. This process can also make the orientation process a lot easier for the more shy among us.

Humility and gratitude

People do not typically appreciate working with arrogant people, or people who aren't open to criticism. These attitudes will make it much harder to make friends, and people will generally try to avoid working with others who project these ugly traits. It is always important that you let your coworkers know that you are open and receptive to criticism and new ideas and it is also important that you avoid stepping on their toes with an arrogant attitude. Thanking people for their work and helping them along the way will also make people more agreeable to you.

Listen and observe actively

In the average workplace, as in anywhere else, it is usually a good idea to gain an understanding of the culture that surrounds you and its norms before criticising it. If you want to keep a good standing with your coworkers and bosses, it is important to show respect for the company and those who work for it. This will not only help you but others around you when they invariably try to emulate your performance, creating a better overall work environment.

Transparency and honesty

It is impossible to work with others without conflict. Not only is avoiding this conflict unsustainable, but it also hinders development. What is always more important is that you are able to deal with conflict productively and maturely whenever it arises. Under these circumstances, it becomes important to take responsibility and to avoid carrying blame too far. You should also never neglect to apologize when it is necessary.

Keep a clear expectation of the work relationship

Goals are usually more easily reached when sought after with planning to an end in mind. You do not have to turn communication with coworkers into some type of Machiavellian mind game, but you should be precise in what you say to others and keep preformed goals in mind when speaking with coworkers at times. This tip is especially useful for managers and bosses. Give the people below you a clear example of what the company wants from them and try to make your demands accessible yet practical. The more clarity that is provided to workers, the more confidence those workers will typically have when meeting the demands placed on them. Workers at all levels should avoid ambiguity when discussing work-related issues with others. It is important to remain objective and practical when discussing these matters, and any other attitude will generally be met with confusion and frustration.

Encourage and engage

Employees work best on a diet of praise and recognition about every two weeks. It is normal to desire being seen through your work and for your work to be acknowledged. It is not just a weightless platitude to assert that praise and recognition carry further among employees than do salaries and benefits, it is the truth. As Maya Angelou said, "people will forget what you said, people will forget what you did, but people will never forget how you made them feel." If you make people feel inferior, lazy, or useless, they are going to remember that you did that. If you make them feel valued, competent, and important, they are likewise going to remember that you did that.

Remember that coworkers are only humans

The expectations that you should place on your coworkers should always be grounded in reality, and erring on the side of minimalism. You only have the right to expect from coworkers about as much as you have to offer, whether that be a lot or a little. Try to always remember that your coworkers, whoever they might be, are just as human as you are. With that being said, it becomes important to come to know the people working around you. You should try to come to know what interests, hobbies, personal lives, dreams, and aspirations they have. Allow them their privacy, but show them that you take a personal interest in their happenings. The more that you do this, the stronger bonds and relationships you will develop. Getting to know who works around you can make not only your work life but also your own inner life all the more meaningful.

Embrace differences between individuals

It is easy to underestimate the difficulty in getting to know new coworkers. It can be very intimidating or even frustrating to go through this process, especially with coworkers who can be disagreeable or tyrannical. These are normal issues to confront though, and ones that never go away. Knowing how to deal with these people and situations can be tricky, as there are no manuals or textbooks that teach how to, but erring on the side of professional courtesy is a must. Seeing the people you work with more as humans and less as coworkers is always beneficial in supporting strong relationships. As humans, those who you work with are bound to differ from you in a wide variety of ways. Always be respectful of those differences, as they are usually good things for you to be around. Also, in modernity, it is important to remain cognizant of your own conduct at every moment of a workday.

Develop your people skills

As you already know, good relationships start with good people skills. These are otherwise known as "soft skills." Some examples of soft skills that are advantageous to have in the workforce are leadership skills, proclivity toward teamwork, problem-solving skills, communication skills, flexibility/adaptability, work ethic, and interpersonal skills. All of these skills have one common theme: sociability. Without being sociable with your coworkers, you can never expect to build and maintain good relationships with them, nor can you expect to build and maintain your career. If you are not sociable, then you may remain at the bottom of every work hierarchy that you find yourself in, or you may not even be able to keep work.

Identify your relationship needs

This one is closely related to the one on keeping a clear expectation of the work relationship, but it is also important to be clear with yourself and others about what you need to work properly. It is not fair to let yourself get bullied into relationships and situations that do not work in your favor. You have a right and an obligation to serve your own best interest, and this can be done effectively without making other people around you suffer. The first step in doing this, however, is specifying your needs. This is most easily done by journaling on what bothers you and brainstorming methods of fixing the issues at hand. Once skills in doing this are developed, they can be applied to any and all facets of your life, it just takes the initiative to get this ball rolling.

Schedule times to build relationships

Scheduling a time period is one of the best things that you can do for yourself in the contemporary world. This is also true for building relationships. Even if the time each day is minuscule, 5 to 20 minutes, for example, over time this practice can and will help to improve the relationships with your coworkers.

Appreciate your coworkers

If there is one thing that everyone who you ever work with is always going to want, it is an appreciation for the work that they do. If you keep in mind that everyone else is doing more or less as much as you are doing then appreciating them becomes much easier. Showing that you are thankful for the work that others have to offer will invariably open the door to better relationships and even boosted company morale.

Positivity is important

Focusing on remaining positive will not only help you with your mood and well-being, but it will also help those around you. Positivity is a trait that is attractive and contagious, and it makes working (and living) much easier and enjoyable. Negativity, on the other hand, is repellent and leads only to further suffering. Remaining positive not only improves your relationships with your coworkers, but it also boasts many health benefits, including lowered heart rate and blood pressure, a strengthened immune system, lower levels of cortisol and blood clotting, less muscle strain and heartburn, lower levels of chronic pain and disease, and even a longer average lifespan. With all things considered, a person really can't even afford negativity.

Controlling and managing boundaries

Managing boundaries becomes important when there are uneven distributions of time and energy being spent on the people and things that you work with. For example, if one coworker of yours wants to speak with you for hours out of every day while another never speaks to you, it could be a good idea to close that gap. While working, it is never a pleasant feeling to be spread thin. Meanwhile, it is ill-advised to neglect to keep enough on your plate. To maintain balance boundaries sometimes need to be set. It is important to be assertive while doing this also. If you cannot afford certain social interactions, then there is no shame in turning them down politely.

Gossip is a destructive force

The biggest killer of workplace companionship is usually gossip. This is also the most cowardly means of getting your points across, and it should be avoided at all costs. When an issue with a coworker arises, it is always important to address it directly with the coworker in question and usually no one else. Playing office politics often ends badly for all parties involved and seldom gets any problems solved.

Active listening

When a person speaks, they want reassurance that they are going to be listened to. If they are not listened to, then there is no reason why they should speak and, just like that, a coworker becomes ostracized and alienated. This is why it is important to listen actively to what a coworker says and to absorb the contents with an open mind. If you do this, people will be more inclined to trust you, and you will become more admired at your place of work.

Improving workplace relationships can be one of the most difficult aspects of keeping a job but, if done effectively, it can make working much easier and more enjoyable. It can be pretty surprising to see just how quickly things in a workplace can plunge into chaos if these steps, or others like them, are never taken by anyone. Once plans for improving relationships are administered within a workplace, however, the whole of the company improves, yourself included.

Chapter Two: Controlling Emotions

The workplace can be one of the most difficult places to control emotions in. No matter how hard you try, those difficult days are always bound to come up. In your personal life, your reactions to stressful situations are much more free, but in the workplace, your reactions are subject to the scrutiny of your coworkers. Any emotional outbursts while working can not only damage your professional reputation and productivity, but they can even get you fired.

Under normal circumstances, it is usually easy to maintain composure in the workplace, but under more stressful circumstances, such as staff layoffs, budget cuts, and department changes, staying calm can prove difficult, if not impossible. Under these circumstances, however, it becomes even more important to keep your temper, as bosses typically consider the demeanor of their employees when deciding who gets laid off. You have complete freedom on how you react to certain situations, but that freedom comes with responsibility, especially in the workplace.

It may seem easy to decide how you're going to react in certain situations with hindsight, but it is always advisable to explore techniques in dealing with these situations and emotions. Here, we will discuss many negative emotions associated with employment, as well as many methods of coping with these emotions.

The most commonly reported negative emotions among workers are as follows:

Worry/nervousness, frustration/irritation, dislike, anger/aggravation, disappointment/unhappiness

And now we will get into some strategies in dealing with these unhealthy emotions.

Worry/nervousness

These are two of the most unpleasant and unhealthy emotions on the spectrum, and, unfortunately for workers, these two emotions plague virtually every workplace. This anxiety can stem from a number of sources: fear of getting laid off, social problems, low salaries, large workload, and so on, and be compounded with problems at home, or with family or friends. A small amount of stress can be a productive thing, but once it becomes chronic anxiety, health problems start to occur. Here are some tips on how to avoid excessive anxiety:

Break cycles of worry

Do not surround yourself with anxiety. If you can foresee needless anxiety stemming from a situation or a conversation, avoid that anxiety. Try to minimize the number of anxiety inducing things that you have to deal with.

Try deep breathing exercises

These help primarily to slow down your breathing and heart rate. There are all sorts of different deep breathing exercises that you can learn about on the internet. For one, there is cyclical breathing, breathe for 4 seconds followed by holding for 4 seconds, and then out breaths for 4 seconds followed by holding for 4 seconds. When doing these exercises, it is important to focus on your breathing and nothing else. In addition to these exercises, there are other physical relaxation exercises that will help reduce workplace stress, including progressive muscle relaxation.

Focus on improving the situation

Whatever it is worrying you in regards to work, brainstorming solutions and making attempts at them will help reduce your anxiety. Doing these things will also make you a more valuable asset to your company.

Journal your worries down

Simply writing down the things that bother you will do a lot to alleviate the anxiety surrounding them. This technique also helps to curtail sleep problems and nightmares, as worries that we write down during the day don't typically bother us by night. Once these are written down, you can then schedule times to deal with these issues. Before that time comes, let these issues leave you and go about your day. When that time comes, make sure to perform a proper risk analysis before putting any plans into place.

Worry and nervousness can decrease self-confidence and lead to health complications. it is always important to trail these negative emotions away and remain confident and secure.

Frustration/irritation

Frustration is more often than not caused by the feeling of being trapped or stuck at a point that you want to get out of, but cannot. This feeling can be caused by a number of things, especially at work. A colleague blocking a project of yours, a boss too disorganized to catch a meeting on time, or a phone call held out longer than necessary are just a few examples that come to mind. Frustration, whatever its causes, should always be dealt with quickly because when it is not, it can accumulate into anger and other even more negative emotions.

There are, however, many ways of dealing with this awful emotion, a few of which are listed below:

Stopping to evaluate

The best thing to do when feelings of frustration arise is to stop what you are doing and take the time to evaluate them. Writing your frustrations down in this stage can help. After this is done, think of some positive aspects of your current situation. This will improve your mood and reduce further frustration.

Look for positive things

Again, finding silver linings in a frustrating situation will make you see the events unfolding in a new light. This change in your thinking will improve your mood, among other things. If it is a person who is causing you frustration, then keep in mind that it is probably not personal, and if it is an event or situation, then it can probably be solved. Try to move on from this step as much as possible.

Recall the last time you felt frustrated

If you can remember the last thing that you were frustrated about, then you can probably remember how that thing eventually resolved itself. Looking at things with hindsight, they always work out fine. You can also probably recall that your feelings of frustration did not do much to help you in that last situation, so to assume that they are helping you this time around would not be very prudent. Perspective is everything, and so many issues lose so much of their stature when seen from different angles.

Dislike

Dislike for certain coworkers is inevitable, and when it pops up, it seldom goes away. We all have to work with people who we dislike at one point or another, so when these people arrive, it is important to take steps toward dealing with them responsibly. Some of the best things that you can do in these situations are to:

Show respect

You are never obligated to get along with everyone you work with, but you are, in many ways, obligated to show them all respect. When these situations arise, pride and ego are two things which you should set aside, even if the other party(s) are not willing to. This will allow you to come out of the experience with your dignity intact, whatever the outcomes may be.

Be assertive

If a coworker is rude or unprofessional to you, do not be afraid to tell them so. If you do so with certainty and fairness, they might be inclined to change some of their attitudes and behaviors in the future.

Anger/aggravation

Anger is arguably the most destructive emotion contained in a human. This is especially true when the anger is out of control in the workplace. It is also an emotion which most of us do not handle very well. As far as work is concerned, there is typically very little room for anger, which is problematic because much of it then gets taken home with us. Controlling this emotion is one of the most important steps in keeping any given job, especially for those who have difficulties with this. Some tips for dealing with this emotion are listed below:

Watch for the early signs of anger

No one else can detect when your anger is building up quite like you can, so detecting it early is your own responsibility. As was mentioned before, you decide how to react to situations, so if you react in anger, no one holds accountability for that happening.

When anger arises, take a break from what you are doing. When you start to get angry, closing your eyes and trying the aforementioned deep breathing exercises can help you hugely. These actions will do a lot to interrupt your angry thoughts and help to put your mind back on a more positive, relaxed pathway, reducing irrational statements and decisions made.

Picture yourself when you get angry

Imagining how you look and behave will usually give you some well-needed perspective on the situation at hand. For example, if you have the urge to shout at a coworker, think about what you would look like doing so: flustered, mean, and demanding. With that imagery in mind, it is easy to see that you would not be a good coworker in making that decision.

Disappointment/ unhappiness

Disappointment and unhappiness are two of the more pullulated emotions in modern workplaces. These two are almost equal to anger in their unhealthiness; in fact, unhappiness may be unhealthier. These can also have detrimental impacts on your productivity, as they can leave you feeling exhausted and drained, and also less inclined to take risks in the future. Here are some steps that can be taken to curtail the effects of these awful emotions.

Consider your mindset

Try to always keep in mind that things will not always go your way. If they did, then life would become prosaic and meaningless. It is, sometimes, the adversity and the suffering that give life its meat. Do not try to avoid these things, the answer to these problems lies in the willingness to confront them.

Set and adjust your goals

Disappointment can often stem from neglecting to reach a goal. This rarely means, however, that the goal is no longer reachable. It is natural to feel disappointment in these situations, but you must always find the willpower to pick yourself back up. You could, for example, keep your goal, but just make a small change. Anything that will help you to get past the disappointments that you face.

Record your thoughts

One method for dealing with negative emotions is to write them down. When you feel unhappy or disappointed, try writing down what is bothering you, and be specific about your concerns. Is it your job that is bothering you? A coworker? Do you have too heavy of a workload? Writing these concerns down will help you to single out what exactly is bothering you and how you can improve on these areas of concern. Remember that you always have more powers than you think in improving a situation.

Remember to smile

Forcing a smile onto your face can actually make you feel happier and relieve stress. In addition, this activity also releases the neurotransmitters dopamine, endorphins, and serotonin, which all lower heart rate and blood pressure. The endorphins released also act as natural painkillers, and the serotonin acts as a natural antidepressant. Smiling will also make you look more attractive to those around you, further bettering the relationships you have with your coworkers.

Now that the main emotions that have adverse effects on most workers have been covered, let's take a look at some more strategies for dealing with these:

Compartmentalize your stressors

Try to keep stress and baggage from work and home in those respective places. You can use mental techniques, such as imagining the stressors locked away in a box for the time being. If you do not try to compartmentalize these issues, then waters will get very muddied up in your personal life, and things will become very complicated.

Identify your own self-talk

Relay to yourself what you tell yourself. By doing this, you may find yourself repeating thoughts and phrases to yourself that are not necessarily true or helpful. Try to identify your own thoughts that may be misleading or based on thinking errors. Doing this will help you move on from some of your worse points and attitudes into a more productive and expansive mindset.

Identify and accept your emotion

There is virtually nothing you can do to control an emotion that you are not even willing to come to terms with having. It is like denying the existence of a spider right in front of your eyes, the spider will just get bigger and bigger until it is all that you can see. In identifying what emotion(s) you are having and accepting that they are a natural part of life, you are taking lots of power away from them. In doing this, you are also becoming a greater solver of your own problems.

Affirm your rights

There are many places in life, work especially, where you are bound to feel like you have no rights and no control over what happens to you. By identifying your rights and your powers, you are giving yourself some perspective on the things that are in and out of your control. After taking some time to do this, you may find that you are much more powerful than you think you are. This will improve your mood and your self-confidence to affirm these rights that you have.

Communicate strategically

Anyone can drone on about the things that they do not like, but it takes skill and grit to actually get things done to fix all their problems. When you are trying to communicate with others, especially disagreements, it is always important to be precise in your language. This will allow you to communicate your qualms more effectively, and it will also decrease the chance of having misunderstandings and heated arguments. When trying to get a point across, try to come into the situation with some idea of what you want to get accomplished and your probability of having a productive conversation will increase dramatically. If others reply emotionally, let them vent and be understanding. You may learn more from them than they will from you. Ask for more details as well, and the two of you will probably come closer to an understanding because of it.

Be objective

Try to look at whatever is bothering you from both analytic and synthetic approaches. An analytic approach will help you understand the one issue with more depth and clarity, while a synthetic approach will help you understand the issue within the class of all of your possible issues. It is important to look into things with depth and focus, but seeing things as parts of your whole understanding will help you to make connections and find out why these certain things bother you through free associations.

Emotions are never right or wrong, they are only felt. There is no shame in feeling emotions unless of course, the emotion is shame. Emotions will always come and go and are always wiser than the ego. Each one of us, however, has free will in how we react to life's vicissitudes. Controlling emotions is not always easy; in fact, sometimes it becomes nearly impossible. But this skill is just like any other in that it can be improved with practice and diligence.

Chapter Three: Building Confidence and Finding Long-Lasting Success

Low self-esteem is one of the most detrimental traits a person can have to overall well-being. One of the trickiest things about this trait is that it can be very deeply rooted in negative childhood experiences and then compounded by more negative experiences later in adulthood, such as ill-health, getting a divorce, losing a job, toxic relationships, or a general sense of having no control.

Low self-esteem can also increase the likelihood of developing mental health disorders and the severity of their effects. This trait has a complex and often comorbid relationship with disorders such as borderline personality disorder and depression. In depression, for instance, the disorder of depression can lead to a lowering of self-esteem, which in turn can lead to more depression. This is a destructive personality trait that can work with so many other factors to damage and destroy you.

Those who suffer from low self-esteem often view the world as a very hostile and unwelcoming place and themselves as its victim. This is not a great worldview to take, as people who see the world in this way are often reluctant to assert and express themselves. They then miss out on valuable opportunities and experiences that they otherwise would have had, feeling powerless to live life to its fullest. This creates yet another systemic loop of missing out on life, followed by feeling more and more inferior. It is easy to get caught up on this, but sometimes very hard to get out of it.

Here are some tips and techniques on how to build your confidence and avoid the systems of self-degradation that low self-esteem can cause:

Make two lists: one listing your achievements, and one listing your strengths

It may be beneficial to include a second party in this process, as low self-esteem can morph our self-perceptions to a point at which it becomes impossible to be objective when qualifying ourselves. Doing this will immediately make you feel more confident and ready to take on the day's challenges. It will also give you some perspective on where your personal development is at. This is a great means of boosting self-esteem and finding out what traits you possess that you can use to your advantage in the future.

Look at yourself in a more positive light

You have intrinsic value. You are a unique person, and there is something sovereign about you. You are the architect of your life, you build its foundations and choose its contents. It is important to remind yourself of these things throughout life. Looking at yourself through a positive light is the only way you can afford to look at yourself, and it makes life so much easier. When negative thoughts such as “I am a loser” or “no one wants me around” come to mind, it is your responsibility to identify and challenge those thoughts. Treat yourself like someone who deserves to be purged of thoughts like those, because they never help you.

Pay more attention to your personal hygiene

Take regular showers, brush your teeth, clip your nails and so on. Outside appearances are known to affect self-concept.

Wear only clean clothes that make you feel confident

Try wearing the clothes that you think you and the others around you will like the best. Consider throwing out some of your old, worn-out clothes for newer, better clothes.

Eat good foods as part of a healthier, more balanced diet

The benefits of doing this are innumerable. This tip should be followed above all others listed here. You should also make mealtime an especially mindful and relaxing time, taking time to enjoy every moment. This is also the time of the day when your senses are most active.

Exercise regularly

This is another incredibly important tip. Set some time away each day, say 20 to 30 minutes, for a brisk walk or a bike ride. In addition, it could help to set aside time 3 to 4 times a week for more vigorous forms of exercise. These could be weight lifting, team sports, martial arts, and so on. This will not only increase your self-esteem, but it will also reduce your risk of chronic disease, increase your energy levels, and even improve the functioning of your brain.

Get enough sleep at night

This is a big factor in living a healthy life that all too often gets ignored by modern people. Getting an appropriate amount of sleep each night (7 to 9 hours) can not only boost your mood and your self-esteem, but it can also reduce your risk of developing heart disease and/or high blood pressure. Doing this also makes your waking life more enjoyable and productive.

Reduce levels of stress

There are many different means of doing this. Deep breathing exercises, exercise, and venting to others come to mind. This will increase your confidence because, in part, of all the things that you will accomplish, you will increase your energy.

Make your living space clean, neat, comfortable, and attractive

Seeing clutter, dirt, and general disorganization activates the same neural pathways that seeing predators like snakes and spiders activates. You also feel about the same in the two instances, flustered and uncomfortable. This is why it is wise to keep your living space tidy, to clear up your mind if nothing else.

Do the things that you enjoy doing more often

This one may be obvious, but taking part in activities that you enjoy will make you much more fulfilled and confident. You can get all of your work done and fulfill all of your obligations in a day and still be able to do the things that you enjoy doing if you are persistent.

Pursue artistic endeavors

Painting, practicing an instrument, writing, dancing, whatever artistic activity you prefer will help to boost your confidence and happiness. It will also reduce your levels of stress. You might even find that you have artistic talents the likes of which you were not aware of. You never know until you try.

Set challenges for yourself that you can realistically meet

Setting goals that are out of your league can be a good way to boost productivity, but they also may reduce your self-esteem if you always expect to meet them. It is advisable to be realistic with yourself when setting your own personal goals. If you are, then you won't feel stretched thin, and you will be able to meet your own expectations more easily.

Get started on some of the things that you have been putting off

Finishing the tasks that you procrastinate on is always a great way to relieve stress and anxiety. It leaves you with free time afterward to relax and unwind. This will also boost your confidence by showing you your own competence and work ethic.

Be nice to people, and do things for them

Being altruistic will not only give you the immediate feeling of joy, but it will also make others appreciate you more, in turn making you even more confident. You will gain the respect of others as well as additional self-respect by behaving in this manner.

All these tips mentioned above should help to boost your self-esteem. This trait is, however, always going to be a work in progress for those of us who have low self-esteem. This is why it is important to stay persistent in fending off these sometimes die hard self-debasing traits and attitudes. Once some confidence has been found, however, it becomes beneficial to know what to do with it. How do you become successful with your new attitude, and how do you maintain that success? Hopefully, these next few tips will help you to answer those questions.

Aim big

This one is thrown around a lot but very rarely adhered to. Michelangelo, a centuries-old ideogram of success, once said that "the greater danger for most of us lies not in setting our aim too high and falling short, but in setting our aim too low, and achieving our mark." This quote holds especially true when imagining if Michelangelo had never become an artist, taking instead a "normal" day job. It is hard to tell where art would be today as a result.

Here we have the idea of hefty goals never being met as preferable to small goals successfully achieved. This is obviously not always the appropriate strategy in goal setting, but as we get older, we tend to lose energy and get a bit more lackluster in our goals and operations. Keeping your ambition is like keeping your youth, you get to retain so much of your potential and energy. So many people place realism over their aspirations, which is fine for them, but it should be noted that there is room for the both of them despite your age or walk in life.

Find what it is that you love to do most and do it

Media mogul Oprah Winfrey once said "you know you are on the road to success if you would do your job, and not be paid for it." This is a great one to consider while at work. If you can imagine yourself being as successful as possible at your current job, you can probably see yourself spending most of your time doing this. If this happens to be a job that you hate doing, then this would mean only spending all your time doing things that you do not enjoy. There is no sense in living like this, so why not instead spend most of your time doing something that you love to do?

If you take this step and success did not meet you, then you still spent all your time doing the things you love to do the most. You also probably learned a lot and developed lots of skills surrounding whatever these activities are. Many people do the things that they love to do most on the side for years, just for the sake of doing those things.

Learn how to balance life well

Phil Knight, the CEO of Nike Inc., once said "there is an immutable conflict at work in life and in business, a constant battle between peace and chaos. Neither can be mastered, but both can be influenced. How you go about that is the key to success." Those who strive greatly for success often make the mistake of placing the object of their success at the center of their lives. While it is important to work hard and to stay on top of your obligations, it is more important to lead an enjoyable life.

Workers tend to think that their job, whatever it may be, may lead them to success if they just work harder. They often work for long hours late into their evenings each day to make success happen. This is ill-advised, however, because whatever gains that come out of it come at the costs of their health, rest, and even their lives being enjoyable. This type of lifestyle burns people out and often makes them resentful as a result. To add to that, the successes that they do gain are usually only marginal. This lifestyle also destroys a worker's personal and social life. It leaves no time to go out with friends and little time to work on personal projects. Maintaining a balance between work and social life is one of the hallmarks of success that needs to be managed carefully and persistently.

Lose your fear of failure

Henry Ford, the founder of Ford motors, once said "failure is simply the opportunity to begin again, this time more intelligently." There is an anecdote of yet another important figure of the industrial revolution in respect to this tip; it took Thomas Edison several hundred failed attempts before he created the first successful light bulb. Afterward, one interviewer asked him "how do you feel after all of your failed attempts?" His response was tactful and wise: "I did not fail, I learned hundreds of ways *not* to invent the lightbulb."

From each and every one of his "failures," he took away a lesson of some sort. From these, he gained perspective on what would and would not work. He used a good attitude and an eye for finding helpful experiences to lead to his eventual success. This is the way that anyone who strives for success must conduct themselves.

The moral of the Thomas Edison story could be to monitor and learn from your own failures and turn them into valuable learning experiences. These will give you better ideas on how and how not to go about your work. You will also learn a lot about the work itself.

Keep your resolution to succeed unwaveringly

Colonel Sanders, the founder of KFC, was once quoted as saying "I made a resolve then that I was going to amount to something if I could. And no hours, nor amount of labor, nor the amount of money would deter me from giving the best that there was in me. And I have done that ever since, and I win by it. I know."

This tip is incredibly important, and it can be used in tandem with the one listed below very effectively. Giving up on your goals after a failure is the easiest thing in the world to do. If the failure is large and devastating enough, it can even seem like the only option. It takes, however, a burning and inextinguishable desire to succeed to curtail these defeatist urges though.

You have to put 100% into the things you go into, or else your plans will always fall through. If you do not give your goals everything that you have then each failure and each setback is going to hurt and dissuade you even more than the last. This will continue until you push back and fight for your dreams with everything that you have.

Success, in whatever form, is a hard thing to achieve. If it were easy to achieve, then everyone would be successful, but it instead discriminates against those who do not work for it. It is not possible to find success without grit and sacrifice, a point which brings us to our last tip on finding long-lasting success.

Be a person of action

Leonardo Da Vinci, one of the greatest geniuses of all time, once observed "it had long since come to my attention that people of accomplishment rarely sat back and let things happen to them. They went out and happened to things." This one will not only lead you to success, but it will also lead you to be mean and to be proud. The world is not kept running by people waiting for things to just happen to them, it is kept running by industrious people taking charge of themselves and the responsibilities they keep. It is useless to sit around and expect magic beans. It is almost always useful, however, to get to work on making your aspirations realities.

The tips and techniques mentioned above should help to bolster your self-esteem and make you more successful. If these goals are important to you, try applying these techniques in your everyday life and see if they work for you.

Chapter Four: Social Engineering and Leadership

The importance of social engineering and leadership are often underestimated by contemporary thinkers. Most people are so absorbed in manipulating and taking down hierarchical structures that they neglect to figure out how to manifest themselves within these structures. Whether you have a proclivity toward leadership or not, it still remains important to have a working knowledge of leadership and how it works among groups of people.

Leaders, above all else, help themselves and others in making steps toward doing the right things. In doing this, they build an inspiring vision, set direction, and create new possibilities. Leadership is, in part, about mapping out the route to your team's successful future. It is challenging, but also exciting, dynamic, and inspiring. Setting the direction of the pack is not the only responsibility of a leader though. They are also obligated to guide their people in these directions in a smooth and efficient way. This may be the more challenging skill which takes more time to develop.

This chapter and its tips on the process of leadership will be based on the "transformational model" of leadership proposed by James MacGregor Burns and further developed by Bernard Bass. This model more so focuses on bringing about change through visionary leadership than the normative managerial processes designed to maintain the current performance of given groups.

An overview of leadership

The following are a few traits of an effective leader:

5. Succeeds in creating an inspiring vision of the future
6. Inspires and motivates people to engage with that vision
7. Manages the delivery of the vision
8. Builds and coaches a team, so that it becomes more effective in meeting the vision

Effective leadership requires all of these traits working together with one another. Next, it would be helpful to explore each one of these elements in greater detail.

Succeeds in creating an inspiring vision of the future

In the workforce, a vision that a boss prognosticates needs to be a convincing, realistic, and attractive depiction of the situation that you want to be in in the future. This vision should set priorities, and provide direction and a marker to people to assure that all are able to see whether or not the goals set forth have been achieved.

To create a reliable vision, leaders must first assess and analyze their current situation to get an understanding of where to go. Some steps that are appropriate to take in this stage are considering the evolution of their industry in the future, considering the behaviors of their competitors, and how to innovate successfully to shape their business for competition in the future marketplace. The next step is to undergo some scenario analysis to assess the validity of their vision.

Leadership is, therefore, proactive rather than reactive; looking ahead, problem-solving, and constantly evolving.

Once a leader's vision has been developed, it is necessary to sell the vision. To do this, they have to make the vision compelling and convincing. A compelling vision allows people to understand, embrace, see, and feel it. Effective leaders can communicate their visions effectively and clearly. They are able to speak about their visions in ways that people can relate to, and they inform people in an inspired way. This makes people more receptive to their ideas and more inclined to follow what they have to say.

Shared values and vision creation are two major components of leadership. Those who can develop skills in these two areas are more likely to succeed in leadership roles.

Inspires and motivates people to engage with that vision

The foundation of leadership is a compelling vision. This vision is only met, however, by a leader's ability to inspire and motivate their followers. At the beginning of most projects, it is easier to stay enthusiastic, which in turn makes it easier to win support for it than in other stages of the project. Afterward, the initial enthusiasm fades is when it becomes more difficult to maintain an inspiring vision moving forward. People change along with their attitudes and working methods, as well as their goals. Good leadership requires recognizing this phenomenon and working hard throughout a given project to be cognizant of others' needs, hopes, and desires while meeting the vision at hand. It is a juggling act of altruism and pragmatism that helps wherever it goes.

One means of linking effort, motivation, and outcome is known as expectancy theory. This place is an emphasis on leaders linking two main expectations that their followers have. These are listed below:

- The expectation of hard work leading to good results.
- The expectation of good results leading to incentives or rewards.

People with these expectations foresee both intrinsic and extrinsic rewards and therefore work harder to achieve success.

One other approach includes repeatedly restating the vision with added emphasis on its rewards and communicating the vision in a more effective and attractive way.

Expert power is one of the most helpful things that a leader can have. People are more inclined to admire and believe in leaders with this because they are seen as experts at what they do. Expertise comes with credibility, respect, and prestige. This also potentially gives people a right and even an obligation to lead others. Having and displaying competence gives leaders a much easier time motivating and inspiring their followers.

Natural charisma and appeal can also serve as conduits for a leader's motivation of and influence over people, as well as other sources of power. These other sources of power include the ability to assign tasks to people and to pay bonuses.

Managing the delivery of the vision

This area of leadership applies more to management than any of these other tips.

Leaders always need to make sure that they are properly managing the work necessary for delivering their vision. This can be done by either themselves, a manager, or a team of managers delegated by the leader to deliver the vision of the leader.

To achieve this, team members need to meet their performance goals linked to the company's vision. Some means of seeing that this is done are KPIs (key performance indicators), performance management, and project management. One other way of ensuring that the vision is being met is a management style called management by wandering around (MBWA). This style ensures that all the steps that need to be taken are taken in meeting any given goals.

Another trait of an effective leader is the ability to manage change well. Leadership is, after all, constant evolution and adjusting to work's vicissitudes. Managing changes smoothly and efficiently ensures that all goals will be met and obstacles overcome throughout the course of realizing the leader's vision. This can only be done, however, with the backing and support of the people behind the leader.

Building and coaching a team to achieve the vision

Some of the more crucial activities carried out by transformational leaders are individual and team development. Without these, there would be nothing for the leader to lead. The first step in developing a team that a leader has to take is to come to understand team dynamics. There are several popular and well-established models that can describe these to a leader, including

Belbin's team roles approach, and the forming, storming, norming, performing, and adjourning theory of Bruce Tuckman. A more in-depth analysis of this theory is featured below.

Forming

The forming step involves a team coming together at the beginning of a venture to figure out the goals of the group out and how to go about accomplishing these. Members tend to be impersonal and polite during this period as everyone is still getting oriented within the team.

Storming

The storming phase is a bit more selective and critical. In this phase, the leadership may be questioned along with group members ideas. This is very much a culling-off phase of the process as many of the group's members will feel overwhelmed and disconcerted by the turbulence and criticism. Some of them who do not leave after this stage give up on the goal at hand as well. And some just simply do not want to do what is asked of them.

Norming

Norming is the step at which the group comes together to agree on a singular plan for achieving the common goal. In this stage, members of the group are encouraged to yield their ideas for the betterment of the group, and they also come to know and understand each other better, building stronger relationships. It is the working toward a common goal that brings the team members together.

Performing

By the performing stage of the process, the group members are able to work toward accomplishing the goal without very much outside supervision or input. They also come to understand each other's needs better and how to work with one another to accomplish the goal at hand.

Adjourning

In the adjourning stage, the opportunity to reflect on unsuccessful and successful outcomes comes about. Members of the group can use these outcomes to gauge what they should do when working on future tasks. This will help smooth out the process of meeting a goal in the future.

The next time you find yourself working in a group on a certain task, monitor the group's progress through these stages. Group members tend to move through these stages in all sorts of different orders. They actually rarely happen in the order listed above. If, however, team members are aware of the steps that they are moving through—which they usually are not—then they can typically work through these steps much more efficiently and effectively. Walking yourself through these steps listed above will help you navigate the happenings of your workplace better in the future.

Leadership

A competent leader always does their best to ensure that team members are equipped with all the abilities and skills necessary to do their jobs and achieve the overarching vision. To do this, it is necessary to give and receive feedback on a day-to-day basis, as well as to train and coach team members on a regular basis as well. These steps will improve individual and team performances dramatically.

Good leaders lead, but great leaders lead and find leadership potential. When leading a team, it is always helpful to find leadership abilities in others, whatever their current positions may be. This paves the way for not only differentiation in hierarchical status, but also for further development beyond the leader's influence or even stay. It can also give a leader a surprisingly helpful example in other competent workers.

The terms "leader" and "leadership" are often misused to describe people who are actually in managerial positions. These people are often highly skilled and have great work-ethics, but that does not necessarily make them great leaders.

Workplaces are all too often hoisted up on people who others consider to be leaders but are actually managers. These managers often do not provide any aspirations or even long-term goals for their team members, which is fine in the short term, but eventually leads to feelings of meaninglessness and even resentment.

The next discussion points that should be delved into would have to be group dynamics and social engineering. These are important realms to know about when entering a new workplace, or any given social setting for that matter. Here we will look into what group dynamics are and what you need to know about them to master them.

Group dynamics

Group dynamics, whether ignored by participants or not, play a major role in any culture, organization, or unit. People with differing ideas and perspectives make these groups up. It is very rare that all people and their ideologies are homogeneous within any given group. It is, in fact, also dangerous. Leaders are looked up to within these groups maintain the unity of purpose and cohesiveness of the unit. The cultural bonds within these units must be developed more at certain times than in others. Once these bonds are developed, the further effort has to be put in to nurture them.

Dysfunction within these groups occurs with alienation among specific members. When a member feels ostracized, there is very little keeping them from acting out in unpredictable ways. This is bound to come up at times and when it does, the leader can struggle to remain objective as the structure of the cohesive unit starts to fall apart. These are usually the worst periods of chaos in the histories of groups. It is these periods, however, that separate good leaders from bad ones.

At all times, if they are understandable or appropriate, the leader or manager must continue to recognize the team member causing the disturbance as an integral part of the group. Further alienation typically leads only to further disturbance. At these times, it would be beneficial for the leader to look at the employee causing the disturbance as being a special employee, one who could use the leader's help or skills, one who remains part of the group, and even one who may be there to teach the leader something. A review of the nature of the communication, power, and corporate climate of the unit would also be beneficial under these circumstances to further understand the team member's point of view and avoid further disturbances in the future.

A leader must also have abilities in objective introspection. It is not advisable or even possible to guide or help others unless these skills are developed. It is putting the cart before the horse. A leader recognizing their own insecurities will be more easily able to perceive and recognize staff dysfunctions as being symptomatic of systematic dysfunctions. The ego will be more open to rationality once personal problems are more specifically addressed. It takes a secure and mature person to decide that their staff is ultimately more important than their own ideas, moving forward.

Once new steps are taken after dysfunctions, much progress can be made, and the company can often be left better off than they were beforehand because of this. The staff can find new means of communication and ways to relate to one another, they can find also find new modes of behavior all together that could even boost their self-esteem or overall well-being. Fortunately, for the leader, everyone at the company could then boast of having a manager with a plethora of newfound ideas and attitudes. All these intricacies and regulations tend to make working in a group very complicated at times, but if all of these steps are stuck to, and everyone pulls their own weight, the benefits of teamwork can be innumerable.

Conclusion

Thank you for making it through to the end of *Emotional Intelligence*. Let's hope it was informative and answered any questions you had previously regarding the subject. The purpose of this book was primarily to supply you with some tools for fostering your emotional intelligence. This is, however, a trait that takes lots of time and effort to improve on. The next steps for you would be to consider looking into any other resources on this subject and seeing if any are a good fit for you.

This book's subject was broad. Emotional intelligence is a wide concept with lots of components, which means that there is a lot of room for improvement. This book mostly covered emotional intelligence through a lens suitable for use in the workplace, but to truly gain skills in dealing with your emotions you have to live a lifestyle, of sorts, devoted to that goal, in and outside of work.

The workplace is a very important place to keep your emotions under control though. Attitudes and demeanors that are acceptable in most of the public arena just aren't in many workplaces. It is always ideal to separate your work life from your home life, of course, but it is even more ideal to keep a demeanor that is acceptable and respectable everywhere you go.

Finally, thank you again for finishing this book. Continue to apply the principles mentioned here in your life, and you are bound to see some positive changes.